P9-BVH-136

Gifted by Their Spirit

Gifted by Their Spirit

Leadership Roles in the New Testament

Eugene S. Wehrli

The Pilgrim Press
Cleveland, Ohio

The Pilgrim Press
Cleveland, Ohio 44115

© 1992 by The Pilgrim Press

Scripture quotations, unless otherwise noted, are from the New Revised Standard Version Bible, © 1989 by the Division of Christian Education of the National Council of the Churches of Christ in the United States of America, and are used by permission. Those references noted RSV are taken from the Revised Standard Version of the Bible, © 1946, 1952, and 1971 by the Division of Christian Education of the National Council of the Churches of Christ in the United States of America, and are used by permission.

All rights reserved. Published 1992

Cover design by Cindy Dolan.
Book design by EastWord Publications Development.

Printed in the United States of America

The paper used in this publication is acid free and meets the minimum requirements of American National Standard for Information Sciences-Permanence of Paper for Printed Library Materials, ANSI Z39.48-1984

97 96 95 94 93 92   5 4 3 2 1

Library of Congress Cataloging-in-Publication Data

Wehrli, Eugene S.
     Gifted by their spirit : leadership roles in the New Testament /
Eugene S. Wehrli.
          p.   cm.
     Includes bibliographical references.
     ISBN 0-8298-0920-1
     1. Christian leadership—Biblical teaching. 2. Pastoral theology—
Biblical teaching. 3. Bible. N.T.—Criticism, interpretation, etc. I. Title.
BS2545.L42W44 1992
262'.1'09015—dc20   92-27962
                                                                    CIP

Contents

Introduction 1

Chapter 1: *Apostles and Evangelists* 9

Chapter 2: *Prophets* 35

Chapter 3: *Teachers* 61

Chapter 4: *Pastors as Shepherds* 81

Chapter 5: *Ministry* 103

Notes 109

87002

Introduction

The New Testament names various leadership roles in the early church. The list of roles is found in several places—1 Corinthians 12, Romans 12, Ephesians 4—and individual roles are mentioned in specific passages. Paul identifies himself as an apostle (Rom. 1:1); John indicates his identity as a prophet (Rev. 1:3; 22:7-10, 18); and the epistle of James, for example, singles out teachers for reference (3:1). In the lists themselves apostles, prophets, and teachers get special position in the most formal way, being named first as well as numbered: "First apostles, second prophets, third teachers; then..."(1 Cor. 12:28). Likewise, Eph. 4:12, reflecting a more developed church structure, also recognizes other identifiable leadership roles in the church—evangelists and pastors. Finally, in the Pastorals and Acts especially, another set of names occur including elders, deacons, and bishops.

Function and Role

Rom. 12:6-8 and 1 Cor. 12:8-10 seem to mention primarily functions and gifts of the Spirit rather than specific roles. The functions, as diverse gifts of the Spirit for all members, are never replaced by the more identifiable persons who, because they perform basic functions in the church in a leadership way, become identified by the specific primary role that they play.

Further, while persons can be identified with a role (and therefore an office), the role is never limited to such persons in the early church but on specific occasions may be filled by all sorts of individuals. The possession of a role never means that the function performed becomes the possession of those in that role. Nor is there any evidence of persons having a leadership role who feel the need to protect their role from being performed by the whole membership of the church. Never does a function for which persons are set apart become the exclusive possession of those persons. The responsibility remains with the church as a whole. The Spirit always is free in the larger community to challenge the function of the individual gifted leaders (as in 1 Cor. 14).

In fact, those who have identifiable and responsible roles seem to derive authority from the community. For example, because prophecy is a function of the whole church, the church identifies individuals as prophets so that the function of prophecy may be responsibly and consistently performed. This guarantees the integrity of the church, but the church does not thereby abrogate its prophetic responsibility. Further, it assumes that other members, on occasion, may be called to very prophetic acts. The same thing might well be said for the other functions in which the church also recognizes leadership responsibilities. God is free in bestowing gifts of ministry but at the same time sets apart specific historical persons for the different gifts of ministry. While there are other functions that on occasion are exercised as gifts of the Spirit, they are fluid and neither established nor always necessary roles.

Christ and Role

Each of these ministerial functions, which God gives to the church at large and for which God sets apart specific historical persons for definite acts of ministry, continues the incarnation. Here all ministries are integrated and historically located in the person of Jesus Christ. There is a sense in which all the leadership roles given in Israel—prophet, priest, ruler, teacher of wisdom, and teacher-rabbi—no matter how diverse in purpose and understanding, are all gathered up and integrated in the person of Jesus Christ. In that process they are also transformed. Subsequently, in the life of the church, various leadership functions result that belong to the new community. Thus, however, they need to be embodied and incarnate in identifiable persons in order to assure that the integrity of the church is preserved for its mission to society. The roles function primarily to equip the whole church for its ministry in society and to carry on the work of Christ. It seems clearly defined, so that the leadership roles have the task of keeping the unique function of the church clear so that the church is decisive in its role in society, both in its call to missionary witness and in its existence as a community led by the Holy Spirit that differs decisively from a community based on natural likenesses. The fullness of the service of God in Jesus Christ is carried by the varied gifts of the Spirit bestowed on the church and embodied in individual roles.

Only one leadership identity derived from the Hebrew religious community is so closely identified with the person of Jesus Christ that it is never shared in the New Testament church—the function of Jesus Christ as high priest. The priestly ministry belongs to Jesus Christ alone. The sacrificial offering and the priestly act that presents it clearly need to be done only once. Jesus Christ is the total and sufficient sacrificial offering that for all time has broken down the barriers that separate persons from God and from one another. Thus, no leadership group is designated as priests in New Testament congregations. Jesus Christ alone is the mediator who breaks down the dividing wall of hostility created by social class, by sin, by guilt, or by other such factors. Therefore, the function of priest is Christ's alone and the priest's work is forever done.

Occasionally, sacrificial and priestly images are used to describe personal acts in the New Testament, but these are always figures of speech illuminating the deed. There is no defined role of priestly ministry in the New Testament. What the church later described as a priestly ministry is unique to Christ. The church is certain that Christ's priestly work is a one-time act (Heb. 7:24-28; cf. 9:11-14, 25-26; 10:10). His work has perfected relationship to God for the church in every time and place.

There are metaphorical uses of the cultic terms that are applied to the church. The moral life is called a sacrifice, living, holy, and acceptable to God (Rom. 12:1; cf. Heb. 13:16). Likewise, drawing on the promise, "you shall be my treasured possession . . . you shall be for me a priestly kingdom and a holy nation" (Exod. 19:5-6), 1 Pet. 2:9 affirms the symbolic priesthood of the new community (cf. Rev. 1:6; 5:10). Anticipating the use of this Old Testament text, the author of 1 Pet. (in 2:5) already describes the church as a spiritual house built of living stones, whose purpose is to be a holy priesthood to offer spiritual sacrifices acceptable to God. As one reads on, however, the sacrifices the holy priesthood offers are symbolic ones—that is, good conduct among the Gentiles. This conduct is described in the ethical code from 1 Pet. 2:11 to 4:11. Again, there is no leadership role of priest in the New Testament; that has been completely fulfilled by Jesus Christ: "You were ransomed . . . with the precious blood of Christ, like that of a lamb without defect or blemish" (1 Pet. 1:18-19; cf. Heb. 1:3).

The Scope of the Leadership Roles

Our purpose is to examine the leadership roles in the New Testament. We will see that when the words *apostle, prophet,* or *teacher* were used, there were in the community identifiable marks of and understandings about what such persons did and how they operated. We will seek to understand the communal understanding about these roles. Because of the list in Eph. 4:12, the role of pastor is included as something specifically identified within the limits of the New Testament period. The Ephesians text also lists evangelists. Because this text is second generation, the use of the word apostles now seems to have become limited to the founding apostles and was restricted to first generation persons close to Jesus and the founding events. The identification of evangelists in Ephesians, as the study will show, designates persons who carry on the same function originally assigned to apostles without the sanctity that has now gathered around Paul and the Twelve.

Eduard Schweizer points out that there were a wealth of ideas for office in the Greek language: *arche,* "being at the head, ruling"; *time,* "position, dignity"; *telos,* "the completed power of office"; *leitourgia,* "a citizen's voluntary work for the community" in Greece and "priestly ceremonial service" in the Septuagint.[1] What is surprising is that these terms are not used to interpret offices for church leadership in the New Testament.[2] Again, nothing is restricted to one group of persons, although they have been gifted by their Spirit for their function.

Further, the traditional distinction between universal charismatic ministries (apostle, prophet, teacher) and local administrative ministries (bishop, elder, and deacon) do not seem to hold up at all in the New Testament. Distinction between terms lies rather in the ways now delineated. Bishops, elders, and deacons all express aspects of the pastoral ministry and are gathered within the larger role of pastor.

5

In pursuing the study, several crucial areas will be covered as each role is discussed. If the role is clearly defined, descriptive references should give clues to what the perceived role is about. However, since it was no one's purpose in writing the Gospels, letters, and treatises of the New Testament to describe early church practice or polity, these clues will be indirect, revealed in the way persons function and in what they assume as they deal with the issues of faithfulness in the community. And because the roles and persons performing them are identifiable, there ought to be products, even literary deposits, in the New Testament that belong to the functioning of each group. The identification and analysis of these literary products will be important for discerning the assumptions and responsibility of each of these groups. This book seeks to identify how each role functioned as to audience, type of communication, the goal sought and its meaning for Christian life, the situation in the community addressed, the content of communication, the authorizing reality for the role, the way the role is practiced, and the aspect of the ministry of Christ.

The Community

Finally, leadership existed only for the sake of the community. The church was centered around table companionship where all were one in a common loaf (1 Cor. 10:16-17). While there were leadership functions given to persons for the sake of the common good (1 Cor. 12:6), nevertheless, there was no hierarchy or gradation of persons. There were no holy offices or persons. All were saints set apart in one way or another for the service of God.

However, the church did require various leadership functions to be maintained for its own integrity and character, so there were leaders from the beginning—the Twelve, the Seven, or "those who . . . have charge of you" (1 Thess. 5:12). The Spirit sets aside persons who have the gifts needed for the service of

God in the life of the world. Some roles may vary in time and situation in order to maintain the church's wholeness, but others seem constant for the character of the New Testament church— namely apostles, prophets, and teachers.

1

Apostles and Evangelists

An apostle is "one who is sent." That is the etymological meaning of the word, and that functional meaning is borne out in its use in the biblical community. The community is in touch with the image in this title so that the community innately knows what the word means. The self-understanding of being sent raises several implications. An authoritative sender is implied; one goes in another's behalf. Being sent implies some sort of mission or goal—one is to carry or accomplish something for the sender.[1] And being sent implies destination as being sent to someone or to somewhere.

Apostleship

While this image has a broad application for the New Testament community, we do need to make several beginning clarifications, since so much of our knowledge about apostles is communicated through the person and the writings of Paul. Further, Paul so dominates our understanding of the term apostle in the early New Testament that we will have to exercise care to see if we can discern the communal understanding and that of the apostle. In this light several observations are in order. The earliest direct sources for discerning the meaning of apostleship in the New Testament come from the Apostle Paul. We may be able to discern earlier community understandings in the traditions he uses and reflects. At some points Paul personally modifies the apostolic understanding. Later New Testament writings reflect a continued development in the understanding of apostleship. The first part of the canon was the collection of the letters of the apostle. Apostolic identity is basic to the canon of scripture.

Apostles in the Pre-Pauline Tradition

Let us see what basic perspectives become clear when we look at Paul's inherited assumptions about apostleship. Since nowhere does he discuss apostleship directly, many aspects of apostleship in the New Testament remain unclear. However, since assumptions reflect that which is common to the speaker and to the hearers, the essential operational understandings about apostles are best discovered by observing that which seems to be self-evident to Paul.

There is a clear, identifiable group that Paul knows as apostles (Gal. 1:19) that has a lineage that goes back to the earliest days of the church (Gal. 1:17). Paul also is called to be an apostle by God (1 Cor. 1:1). The term has specific technical usage.[2] "Are all apostles?" he asks, expecting the answer, "No" (1 Cor. 12:29). He refers to Andronicus and Junia as "prominent among the apostles" and "they were in Christ before I was" (Rom. 16:7).[3] Further, there is a clearly defined function that Paul can call apostleship—it is a gift (Rom. 1:5) and involves definite tasks (1 Cor. 9:1-2; Gal. 2:8).

As the verb *sent* implies, apostles are the itinerant group among the leaders in the New Testament community. Andronicus and Junia are identified as having been kin and prisoners with

Paul. This would imply itinerancy for them, wherever they were imprisoned, as well as for Paul himself.[4] Peter, also identified as an apostle by Paul, is met in Jerusalem (Gal. 1:18) but later goes to Antioch (2:11), goes to the circumcised (2:7-8), and has some identification with Corinth (1 Cor. 1:12). Paul most certainly identifies his own apostleship with itinerancy. Finally, Paul possibly does not see the other apostles in Jerusalem because they are all out on mission (Gal. 1:19).

Apostles have full authority by the commission of the one sending them. In listing types of ministry Paul names apostles first and identifies them as God's first appointment in the church (1 Cor. 12:28). The language describes the creation of a new role by God.[5] The apostles' function has clear priority also in Ephesians where apostles are listed first (4:11).

The primary commission of an apostle comes through a resurrection appearance as reflected in Acts 1:21-26. Schnackenburg makes clear, however, that an appearance does not create apostleship but is confirmatory.[6] The most revealing case is in Paul's discussion stemming from his citation of the kerygmatic formula in 1 Cor. 15:3-8. The risen Jesus is identified to James, then all the apostles, and last of all to Paul. Paul immediately starts talking about his apostleship and its meaning. Fuller finds this list to be the basis of the apostolic mission,[7] even as the appearances to Peter, the Twelve, and the Five Hundred are church-founding. Apostles are the recipients of a resurrection appearance that becomes the impetus for their mission and the basis of their witness.

While death is the curse that destroys relationship, the appearance of the risen Christ is the affirmation of a new relationship of a different order. Through his appearance persons are re-bound in covenant to the new and living Lord. The historic relationship and call to mission that death ended is now binding in a new way. In the earliest pre-Pauline and Pauline traditions, it was enough to list persons to whom Jesus

11

appeared, that is, the newly established relationship with the risen Lord alone was fundamental.

That apostleship for Paul is the consequence of a resurrection appearance is clear when after listing the appearances he immediately begins talking about his calling as an apostle. While he includes himself in the list of appearances, he identifies himself as the least of the apostles, not worthy to be called an apostle. His apostleship, as that of the others, is a gift, indicated by the appearance of the risen Christ to him. By grace Paul is what he is, an apostle, since he persecuted the church of God and hence was "one untimely born" (1 Cor. 15:8). Because appointment is by God in the church, persecuting the church is the most disqualifying thing that Paul could have done as far as apostleship is concerned.

Such unmerited grace as he received bears its consequence, namely that Paul worked harder than any other apostle. Being the recipient of a gift does not lessen responsibility, but it heightens apostolic effort. Yet because of its origin and nature, Paul's work was "the grace of God which is with me" (1 Cor. 15:10 RSV).[8]

A further question remains. What is the hard work of the apostles that God's grace empowered them to do? 1 Cor. 15:11 makes clear that the hard work is *preaching* the gospel. The apostle is sent to carry the gospel, to evangelize. To manifest the gospel in full authority and power is the ultimate task of an apostle. To fulfill this task Paul was forced to travel the whole ancient world in personal hardship and affliction.

Apostles are the witnesses to the kerygma—the story of the death and the resurrection of Jesus—not as objective reporters, but as persons who know of Christ's death for them and who know of the relationship that the resurrection of Jesus renews with them. Hence, they can proclaim that story in such a way that people might respond in faith.

Surprisingly enough, the emphasis in Paul is on the noun *apostolos*, with reference to an identifiable person or group (the word is used twenty-four times in the Pauline literature, not counting Ephesians or the Pastorals). This usage is consistent with the earlier emphasis. Here we see the dominance of this title as referring to persons engaged in preaching as itinerant missionaries. When the verb is employed, though limited in use,[9] Paul stresses the function of preaching. This is the task of the apostle.

The apostle is the bearer of the tradition of God's gracious activity. The gospel becomes alive when the apostle makes the authoritative testimony, which is not eyewitness recounting, but telling the mighty acts of death and resurrection. Paul identifies that tradition both in the words of the Last Supper (1 Cor. 11:23ff.) and in the formula of the preached faith—"For I handed on to you as of first importance what I in turn had received" (1 Cor. 15:3).

Yet carrying the message is not enough. The goal is to lead persons to faith—to discipleship. Only when that happens and congregations are built up is the mission accomplished. The apostolic witness has as its personal goal a living faith. Telling the story, preaching, is not an end in itself. Faith is impossible without the witness. "But how are they to call on one in whom they have not believed? And how are they to believe in one of whom they have never heard? And how are they to hear without someone to proclaim him? And how are they to proclaim him unless they are sent?" (Rom. 10:14-15). To sum up in reverse order: Apostles are sent to preach; preaching has as its content the story of Jesus Christ; and hearing the story of Jesus calls forth faith. Apostolic preaching has only one goal—faith or a faithful congregation.

Paul as an Apostle

It is evident that Paul's unique self-identity lies in apostleship by the way it permeates his writings. Paul begins his letters with a clear statement of his vocational identity. He is "called to be an apostle" (Rom. 1:1), "an apostle of Jesus Christ by the will of God" (1 Cor. 1:1), "an apostle . . . through Jesus Christ and God the Father" (Gal. 1:1). Apostolic identity controls his being. What does he understand by it? As we have seen, apostleship comes by the authority of God. Beyond this general statement, however, let us seek to ascertain what the distinguishing personal marks of apostleship are for Paul. Of course, in many ways, Paul merely reflects the tradition he inherits.

An appearance of the risen Lord is the foundation of Paul's apostolic identity, as we saw in our discussion of 1 Corinthians 15. The appearance gave him, a persecutor, a relationship to the risen Christ that was the basis of his authority to evangelize.

Likewise, in Galatians, where he is defending the gospel, he makes clear that a revelation of Jesus Christ is the basis and authority of his apostleship. That revelation is described as God "was pleased to reveal his Son to me" (1:15-16). Paul's authority is based in that appearance. To keep the Galatians from continuing to claim his words were only of human origin, he concludes, "I did not confer with any human being, nor did I go up to Jerusalem to those who were already apostles before me" (Gal. 1:16-17).[10] Relationship with Jesus Christ, rooted in an appearance of the risen Christ, is the basis of authority.

A second identifying mark of apostleship that Paul addresses is the formation of a community of faith. When defending himself as an apostle in 1 Corinthians 9, in addition to assertion of a direct revelation of Jesus, he adds a second qualification, "Are you not my work in the Lord? If I am not an apostle to others, at least I am to you; for you are the seal of my apostleship in the Lord" (1-2). Paul is an apostle only in relation to congregations that have been formed in his ministry. This claim may also give us our best functional definition of apostleship. Apostles are those commissioned by God for church planting. The creation of a community of faith is the sign of Paul's apostleship. He has preached the gospel and it has brought forth a community of faith. He is an apostle to Gentiles. The goal has been achieved. Paul, as apostle, is a community founder—the formation of a new congregation was crucial.

Schmithals finds this requirement to be a Pauline development in answer to the Gnostic challenge. For them the apostle's proof of authority must not be based in the past (to have seen the risen Lord), but it must be a present, ecstatic experience. While Paul indicates that he knows such experience, he rejects it as the ground of his own apostolic authority. He refers to the signs of a true apostle (2 Cor. 12:12), but he does not include enthusiasm as a sign; rather the calling forth of a congregation (10:15) and his presence in weakness are the true qualifications of an apostle (11:7; 12:9-10).[11]

The reality of the congregation may also counter another claim some apostles use for authority and which Paul rejects as irrelevant, namely, the practice of carrying letters of recommendation (2 Cor. 3:1). For Paul the only recommendation is a *faith community, called forth by the life-giving Spirit*— "You yourselves are our letter, written on our hearts, to be known and read by all; and you show that you are a letter of Christ, prepared by us" (3:2-3). In this vein it is interesting that Paul has no great story to tell of his "conversion," or of great visions, nor does he have a sheaf of testimonials to his marvelous successes in local congregations. The gospel of Christ is served when the power of God is professed, and that power most clearly works, not through great personages, but in faithful congregations.

While, at times, Paul talks of his work as foundational in the formation of communities of faith upon which others may build (Rom. 15:20; 1 Cor. 3:10-15), Paul also talks about his own work as building up the community (2 Cor. 10:8; 13:10). Here the image is fit into the prophetic pattern that God's ultimate purpose is to build and not destroy (Jer. 1:9b-10; 24:6; 31:28; Isa. 49:17). Paul's apostolic identity also requires him to build up, not destroy, those congregations that he has established. That is his purpose in continually being present with them through visits and through letters carried by his personal companions. The companions and the opportunity to read the letters in the community, evidently repeatedly, are his means of building up the community.

A third aspect of apostleship in 1 Corinthians 9 seems to distinguish Paul's exercise and understanding of the apostle's role from that of the community in general. Most apostles, as great persons, make demands; but Paul was gentle and affectionately desirous of the welfare of his people (1 Thess. 2:6-7; 2 Cor. 11:7-11). Apostles have and exercise the right to be fed and be supported. The record of the teaching of Jesus makes this very clear—"Remain in the same house, eating and drinking whatever they provide, for the laborer deserves to be paid" (Luke 10:7). However, the fact that Paul does not exercise his right has led some to question his very apostolic identity. Paul argues for his right as an apostle to support (1 Cor. 9:1-10) but then indicates that he does not use this right in order not to put an obstacle in the way of the gospel of Christ (9:12). In preaching the gospel Paul is only doing what he is compelled to do. He has no freedom of choice in preaching and therefore no personal merit at this point. Thus, doing it without charge is his grounds for boasting, since he does not insist on his own rights. He lives by his own words, " 'All things are lawful for me,' but not all things are beneficial" (1 Cor. 6:12).

The unique definition of apostolicity by Paul lies in the contrast he makes between himself and those who would be superapostles in Corinth. Paul does not contest their right to the name apostle, as if it were restricted to a few, but he opposes them in terms of the quality of their work. While the term apostle primarily identifies one who is sent with full authority, the word also reflects the role of preacher of the gospel. The question is whether they preach the gospel truly and manifest the signs of an apostle in their lives. Clearly, the superapostles boast in their revelations, put on airs, and stress their superior religiosity. Paul defends himself by boasting also, but his boasting is not in his prestige or religious experience, but in his weakness—the power of the gospel made known in "littleness." Paul is sent to preach "not with eloquent wisdom, so that the cross of Christ might not be emptied of its power. For the message about the cross is foolishness to those who are perishing," and "we proclaim Christ crucified, a stumbling block to Jews and foolishness to Gentiles" (1 Cor. 1:17-18, 23).

Apostles are manifest in weakness and humility. Here we seem to be at the heart of the unique Pauline interpretation of apostleship arrived at from his own struggle, perhaps with Corinth. "God has exhibited us apostles as last of all, as though sentenced to death, because we have become a spectacle to the world . . . in disrepute . . . hungry and thirsty . . . persecuted . . . slandered . . . the rubbish of the world, the dregs of all things" (1 Cor. 4:9-13). The powerful image here shows apostles as

> wretches brought on at the close of a display in the arena . . . already condemned to death, and are sure to perish by combat with one another, or with gladiators, or with wild beasts. . . . This is indeed a position of privilege . . . for it is the position of Christ himself: by their human fortunes as well as by their preaching the apostles placard Christ crucified.[12]

This understanding echoes the origin of Paul's apostleship, which we examined: "For I am the least of the apostles, unfit to be called an apostle" (1 Cor. 15:9). It also is echoed in 2 Corinthians where Paul has been upstaged by the superapostles who have no weakness to confess (chap. 11). They boast of their prowess and have convinced the Corinthians. In order to fight fire with fire, Paul has engaged in an extensive act of boasting (chap. 12). Yet, Paul knows that such a defense of his apostleship ("I am not at all inferior") counters the basis of true apostleship. "I have been a fool! You forced me to it" (12:11). He indicates that he did not burden the Corinthians with demands and arrogant claims. They would have thought him somebody if he did that, but that is not apostolic grounding that is always the power of

God made known in the midst of human frailty. The true apostle points to a transcendent reality beyond self. The apostle is an instrument of a power beyond, not the essence of spirituality.

Paul always speaks of his weakness when he speaks of power so that it is evident that it is the power of God that is under discussion. In 2 Cor. 10:3-5 Paul makes the surprising contrast of human flesh and power. Schutz observes that Paul, in opposing the superapostles' spirituality, rejects the claim that human spirituality is equal to the power of God and that flesh equals weakness. Paul is much too historically rooted for that. He belongs to the human arena (flesh), but he is not therefore unspiritual. Rather it is in the very human weakness that the power of God is made known. While Paul is not spiritual in the way that opponents and society speak, he is the one in whom the power of God can work because he makes no claim for himself in weakness. In his vulnerability the power of God shines forth most brightly.[13] All of this is reflected in the unimpressive presence of Paul (2 Cor. 10:10).

The suffering of the apostles, as a means by which the transcendent power of God is made known (2 Cor. 4:7-12), reflects the eschatological character of the apostles' role. The apostles' power is that of the new age that is being brought into being in the new community. Yet what is powerful in that age is weakness in the old order (cf. 1 Cor. 1:18-4:21). The suffering is a sign that the apostle stands in the old age as herald of the new.[14]

While Paul has a special appointment and task, in no way does that elevate him above the community. It was just this very thing that characterized the superapostles who put on airs. Paul is present as weak; he identifies with the community: "All of you share in God's grace with me" (Phil. 1:7), "What then is Apollos? What is Paul? Servants through whom you came to believe, as the Lord assigned to each" (1 Cor. 3:5). Paul associates himself thoroughly with the others in his greetings. Apostleship is one form of expressing service to God. For the superapostles, ecstasy gained them higher understanding and elevated them to a new level of superiority. For Paul apostleship was one of the gifts that was needed so that the whole community might become a living body of Christ (1 Cor. 12:4-6). When this happens, the congregation is subject to Christ, not to the founding apostle. The apostle belongs to the congregation, not the other way around. "For all things are yours, whether Paul or Apollos or Cephas . . . all belong to you, and you belong to Christ, and Christ belongs to God" (1 Cor. 3:21-23; cf. 2 Cor. 4:5). "Was Paul crucified for you?" he asks a congregation that is making too much of its founders (1 Cor. 1:13).

Paul opposes all forms of spiritual control with corresponding subordination of the congregation. "I do not mean to imply that we lord it over your faith; rather, we are workers with you for your joy" (2 Cor. 1:24; cf. 1 Cor. 7:23; Philem. 14). In approaching a strange congregation he longs to impart a spiritual gift "to strengthen you—or rather so that we may be mutually encouraged by each other's faith, both yours and mine" (Rom. 1:11-12, cf. Phil. 1:5-7). The congregation must discern in him the presence of the Spirit and follow him in freedom (Gal. 5:1). At best he can recall them to what they once knew (Rom. 6:17) or remind them of what claims them (Rom. 15:15, 1 Cor. 4:17).[15] The apostolic faith, not the apostle, is foundational.[16] His work is subject to the community. So the exercise of Paul's apostleship is within the formed community as well as for the forming of the community. There his work is tested (1 Cor. 2:10-16).

The itinerancy of a true apostle argues that apostleship is the basic evangelistic role. For Paul it means taking the gospel to areas where it has not yet been established. Apostles are not leaders in a local congregation or local officials. They are the persons of Christ by whom the church is built. It is a universal mission that goes beyond the Jewish role of *shaliach*, one who is commissioned and authorized for a task, that led Paul to his wide geographical interest and, above all, to seek not to build upon another's work.[17] Building upon another's work is needful, as Paul is grateful to Apollos for building on his work (1 Cor. 3:5-15). The concern is that each build on the foundation of Jesus Christ, the one who commissions. Apollos, while close to Paul, is never directly labeled an apostle. He is a waterer, not a planter. Paul, as an apostle, must break new ground. "We do not boast beyond limits, that is, in the labors of others; but our hope is that, as your faith increases, our sphere of action among you may be greatly enlarged, so that we may proclaim the good news in lands beyond you, without boasting of work already done in someone else's sphere of action" (2 Cor. 10:15-16). And "from Jerusalem and as far around as Illyricum I have fully proclaimed the good news of Christ. Thus I make it my ambition to proclaim the good news, not where Christ has already been named, so that I do not build on someone else's foundation" (Rom. 15:19-20).

Indirectly, Paul sees himself to be a keeper of the faith in new congregations that are tempted by an alien culture. His role is to keep the perspective of faith clear. The number of traditional communal confessional forms that occur in his letters, including all the decisive turning points of his structured letter to the Romans, clearly suggests that an apostle is a keeper of the tradition who is responsible for the foundational basis of the congregation. The apostle continues to have responsibility to preach.

Most important of all, Paul's authority as an apostle lies in the gospel and in Jesus Christ. When Paul follows the word apostle with a possessive genitive, as he does four times, the phrase is "an apostle of Christ" (1 Cor. 1:1, 2 Cor. 1:1, Col. 1:1). Once he speaks of being an apostle "through Christ" (Gal. 1:1). Being an apostle means belonging to Jesus Christ.[18] Christ is not in him, but he is in Christ (2 Cor. 13:4). That is, the priority belongs to Christ and not to Paul's identity as an apostle. It is the superapostles at Corinth whose authority is rooted in their "super" experience. When Paul calls persons to imitate him, he does not call attention to himself but to human weakness; the apostle is claimed and empowered by God. Further, apostleship in Paul is always related to Jesus through the title *Christ*. This makes evident what has already been noted, that apostleship is connected to the salvation event. Therefore, the goal of apostleship is the gospel, or preaching the gospel. When Paul speaks of knowing Christ, the identification parallels "the power of his resurrection," with "the sharing of his sufferings." This he further explicates and repeats in the phrase, "becoming like him in his death, if somehow I may attain the resurrection from the dead" (Phil. 3:10-11). The same emphasis has already been put in more personal terms: "More than that, I regard everything as loss because of the surpassing value of knowing Christ Jesus my Lord. For his sake I have suffered the loss of all things, and I regard them as rubbish, in order that I may gain Christ" (3:8). The pattern is:

> Suffering—power of resurrection
> Death—resurrection from the dead
> Loss of all things—gain Christ

Focal in our whole concern is the understanding of what is meant by the gospel of which the apostle is the bearer. For Paul the gospel is both a verb ("to gospel") and a cognate noun (1 Cor. 15:1; 2 Cor. 11:7; Gal. 1:11).[19] Because of the verbal association, even the noun *gospel* has within it the sense of a reality being achieved through preaching (1 Thess. 1:5). The gospel is an action that serves as a powerful process that effects salvation in history (Rom. 1:16-17; 1 Cor. 9:12b; Gal. 1:16). But the gospel is not only an action set in motion by its preaching, it also has a content that can be set forth (Gal. 2:2). It is a reality in which the Corinthians can stand (1 Cor. 15:1) or a reality that Paul and the Philippians share (Phil. 1:5).

For Paul the gospel is not something to be believed—the object of faith—but it is a power and reality to be heard and obeyed (Rom. 10:16). The task of the apostle is to bring about the obedience of faith, and the authority of the apostle is the very authority of the gospel.[20] To fail to guard and share the gospel is to lose one's basis of authority. To preach another gospel is to be fit to become accursed (Gal. 1:8), inconceivable as it is that there is another gospel. The gospel is the authority both for the apostle and for the community of faith that is to receive it (Gal. 1:9). Neither apostle nor congregation are subject to each other, but both are subject to the gospel. Here again, Paul stands alongside the community of faith; both are equally subject to the gospel. Each depends upon and models for the other. Paul shares in the church's faith; the church can learn the gospel in imitation of Paul who must embody it and who must discern how persons "stand in" the gospel.

The definiteness of the function bestowed is indicated further by the three references in Paul to apostleship (noun, *apostle*) that suggest a function, technically conceived and discharged.[21] While three uses may seem limited, this noun is used nowhere else in the New Testament except once in Acts (1:25). Apostleship is a Pauline understanding. First, the role of apostleship is a gift for Paul. It is parallel to grace as a reality that is received (Rom. 1:5). The purpose of the dual gift is "to bring about the obedience of faith among all the Gentiles" (Rom. 1:5).

The second usage in 1 Cor. 9:1-2 suggests that the generation of a faithful community by Paul's preaching at Corinth is the true mark of apostleship. The Corinthian church is the "seal of [his] apostleship in the Lord." A faith community is the preacher's artisanship in the Lord. The apostle alone is no generator of faith. Faith is the work of the Lord through the gospel proclaimed.

Third, Peter too has an apostleship—a clear function identified and bestowed. It is the mission to the circumcised (Gal. 2:8).

In the only other use of apostleship, in the Lucan tradition, two persons are eligible to take the place of Judas in apostleship. The community in prayer opens itself to God's choosing to fill the rank of apostles who are now clearly identified with the Twelve Disciples. The one requirement is that they have been with Jesus and are witnesses to the Resurrection (Acts 1:21-26).

Throughout Paul there are a number of formulary phrases, rooted in the tradition, that further suggest faith as the response to the preached gospel. Since faith comes from hearing the story of God's act, a brief formulary statement of the story can be called "the faith." Paul often uses these confessional formulas of the community. If you "believe in your heart that God raised him from the dead, you will be saved" (Rom. 10:9). Faith is the fitting response to the confessional announcement of the Resurrection since faith is the relationship established by the resurrection appearance. In the same vein, "It [righteousness] will be reckoned to us who believe in him who raised Jesus our Lord from the dead, who was handed over to death for our trespasses and was raised for our justification" (Rom. 4:24-25).[22] The function of apostles is to witness to the life, death, and resurrection of Christ, God's anointed agent. According to Kramer, the title Christ is used in pre-Pauline formulas only in the kerygmatic announcement of God's saving act.[23] Christ designates Jesus' mission in history to redeem all from their sins. This is the reality that apostles recite and tell forth so that faith might abound. Apostles witness to Jesus as the Christ—the one in whom God has acted for the deliverance of all.

In summary this is clear: (1) Apostles do have authority by virtue of the risen Jesus reestablishing his claim upon them. (2) They are witnesses to the death and the resurrection of Christ. (3) God appointed apostles first. The whole church rests on the witness that apostles make. It is the beginning of the gospel in community; it is foundational (1 Cor. 3:10). (4) The foundational character is developed in the next generation of writings as Ephesians makes clear by such phrases as "built upon the foundation of the apostles and prophets, with Christ Jesus himself as the cornerstone" (2:20; cf. 3:5). In Revelation the foundations of the wall of the new city are inscribed with the "names of the twelve apostles of the Lamb" (21:14). (5) The temptation in apostleship is great. References to false apostles are more frequent than to false teachers. Being first has its own liability (Rev. 2:2); the apostle is tempted to confuse the honor. Apostles can both seek and get acclaim as the "super" leaders of the church. (6) True apostles are only those persons who remember their own humble origins, that the message is folly to all who are tempted to be "super" anything in this society, and that the apostle as a witness is always hidden behind that which is proclaimed—the death and resurrection of Jesus Christ.

Finally, trying to decide who are the apostles, or how they are commissioned, or whether Paul is the last, is not nearly as fruitful as seeing apostles as those commissioned by God to call forth faithful congregations and whose work is tested solely by their fruit.

Apostleship in the Gospels

When we look to the Gospels, certain things stand out. Apostleship is basically separated from the total role of the disciples. The understanding of apostles in Mark is clarified when Jesus sent out the Twelve, two by two (6:7), giving them authority over the unclean spirits and to preach the reign of God (6:7, 12-13; cf. Matt. 10:5, 7-8; Luke 9:1-2; cf. 10:1, 9-10).[24] When they return to report, they are called apostles, probably for the only time in Mark (6:30; cf. Luke 9:10; Matt. 10:2).[25]

Since Matthew and Mark do not use apostle again to refer to the disciples, it is clear that the word designates the function of the Twelve only when they are sent on a mission by Jesus. It is not an alternative label for the Twelve Disciples, but it describes them as commissioned by the Lord to preach the reign of God and work its signs.[26]

Typically in the exercise of their commission, the disciples are tempted to misperceive it, seeing it as a conferring of rights

24

and prestige, rather than as a new service to do the will of the one who gave them power. The historical memory is that the disciples did not get this straight until after the Resurrection. So Jesus has to warn the Seventy when they return, "Nevertheless, do not rejoice at this, that the spirits submit to you, but rejoice that your names are written in heaven" (Luke 10:20). Previously, they were tempted to seek first place (Mark 10:35-37 contrasted with 10:42-45), lord it over others (9:34), become protective of their authority (9:38-40), and reject the primacy of the gospel revealed in suffering (8:32-33).

While the sending of disciples as apostles on mission is remembered of the historical Jesus, nevertheless, the commissioning was limited and death broke any claim of Jesus' authority over the disciples, for death breaks the pledged relationship. Here the resurrection appearances become decisive, as we have already seen in the discussion of the Pauline material. In his resurrection appearance as Lord, Jesus reestablishes relationship with his disciples and all that the historical Jesus had commanded now becomes binding upon the disciples. Consequently, the appearance stories renew the Lord's call for the disciples to follow him and engage in mission. Further, now death can never again abrogate the apostolic call of the church to mission (Matt. 28:19; Luke 24:47; John 20:21).

Jesus is not identified by the word apostle in the Gospels.[27] This is in sharp contrast to the roles of prophet, teacher, and pastor. He is the sender; the disciples are the ones sent. The distinction between Jesus and the apostles is kept sharp and clear. He is the *subject* of the gospel: "Christ died for our sins . . . and . . . he was raised on the third day" (1 Cor. 15:3-4). While Jesus does preach the reign of God, he also brings it in by the way he acts, in teaching and healing, and above all in his passion, so that he is the content of the message of the apostles. He is the subject of the good news, not its guardian and bearer. Even though sent by God, he is uniquely the subject of the gospel in a way that no other can pattern.

While the title apostle is not applied to Jesus, in a few passages in the synoptics he is described as sent by God. "Whoever rejects me rejects the one who sent me" (Luke 10:16; cf. 9:48; Mark 9:37; Matt. 10:33; and also Luke 4:43). John develops this theology thoroughly. Jesus' identity is that he is the one sent from God (3:17, 34; 5:36-38; 6:29, 57; cf. 13:3). Some twenty-six of thirty-two occurrences of the word *pempo* describe Christ as the "one who is sent." In almost all of the cases Jesus is described as the one sent by God.[28] His authority lies in the fact that he is the "sent one." This then becomes the way that Jesus gives the disciples identity (13:16). They are the ones who are sent by Jesus and share in his authority as well as in the reception accorded him as a bearer of the gospel. The active uses of this verb have to do primarily with God sending Jesus and secondly with Jesus sending the Holy Spirit (14:26; 15:26; 16:7). The overwhelming emphasis here is on Jesus as the sent one. Such a relation is what gives him authority to send the disciples on mission into the world (17:18).

The other word that John uses for send, *apostello*, occurs almost entirely in the active sense of God sending Jesus. Here God is stressed as the one who sends. God is the "One who is responsible for His words and works and who guarantees their right and truth."[29] God is the originator of Jesus' work (*apostello*); Jesus is the one in whom and by whom God's mission is accomplished (*pempo*).

Here again being an apostle is heady and tempting stuff for the disciples. In his only use of the noun apostle, John relates Jesus' warning: "Servants are not greater than their master, nor are messengers [apostles] greater than the one who sent them" (13:16). The disciples, and especially Peter, are having difficulty accepting the authority that subjects them, yet this authority is also under subjection to God who "had given all things into his hands" (13:3). Instead, disciples are tempted with images of greatness that avoid the humiliation of servanthood.

Because of John's lack of use of the word apostle, it is said that John shows no interest in the office of the apostle. That, however, is to miss the point. The authority of Jesus in John, and the authority of those who are sent by Jesus, lies exactly in the one who sends them. They are on a mission given by God and in that mission they are to loose the gospel into the world, or as John might prefer to say it, they are to *bring the life that God gives* to the world (cf. 5:21; 6:51, 53; 17:2).

In Luke-Acts the identity of the role of apostles is very clear. Those performing that role are identified primarily with the Twelve (Acts 1:26). The term *the apostles* refers to a specific body of persons throughout the narratives. Paul and Barnabas are identified as apostles only twice in Acts (14:4, 14), and the word apostles, which occurred twenty-seven times in the first half of Acts, is completely absent from the second half, where Paul and his traveling companions are the focus of the narrative. This has led some to conclude that for Luke the apostles are basically in Jerusalem and primarily identified with the Twelve. The mission of the Seventy (Luke 10:1) parallels the mission of the Twelve and thus challenges this conclusion since it refers to a much broader mission than Israel. God's word is for the nations. The fact that Luke uses *euangelizo* both of Paul and the Twelve seems to indicate a parallel function. Finally, Acts identifies the ministry of the Twelve as that of the Word (6:2, 4), and Paul is described continuously as one who is preaching the Word of the Lord.[30]

The role is still clearly marked as a gift (Acts 1:2). The apostles are *preachers* of the kerygma (6:2) as well as *guardians* of the faith. They are the *continuers* of the mighty works performed by Jesus (2:42-43; 5:12). They are communal leaders, witnesses to the Resurrection (4:32-37), administrators of offerings (5:2). There is a clear danger that apostles will be diverted from their primary task, which is not charity but preaching the Word so that persons can come to faith (6:2-5). Further, the apostles, as keepers of the story, bestow authority on others who have been identified by the Holy Spirit as possessing attributes to be used in the life and mission of the church (6:6; cf. 8:18). Even Paul appears before the Jerusalem apostles when the church will not believe his conversion (9:27). This capacity of the apostles seems to be the source of the practice of apostles *appointing local leaders* in the church such as deacons, elders, and overseers.

In an excellent article, Rengstorf rejects Haenchen's contention that the election of Matthias to the apostolate shows Luke's concern with the *office* of the apostolate.[31] As he points out, nowhere else in Acts is there an appeal to the Twelve or the apostolate. Yet he agrees that this story is essential to Luke's purpose, since it is the only narrative between the Resurrection and Pentecost. He concludes that the filling of the Twelve, replacing Judas, indicates that the risen Lord's mission still includes Israel in spite of Jesus' rejection. The Twelve still have their mission to Israel as the unchanged goal, and if "Luke lets the Twelve as a whole disappear from the stage; he wants to make known that after the outpouring of the Holy Spirit questions of organization are of secondary importance for the church, because through the Holy Spirit the risen Lord himself leads and governs the church."[32]

Matthew makes the church's understanding of apostolic authority clear in his telling of the incident at Caesarea Philippi (16:16-19). Simon has received a revelation from God, which is at the base of his confession. Consequently, he is to be the foundation (rock) in the *building* of Christ's church. This is also the basis of his authority in the church.

In the few references to apostle in the pastoral Epistles, the speaker, casting Paul in the traditional role, parallels preacher and apostle, showing a remembrance of that function. In addition, reflecting the development in Acts 2:42, the role of apostle-preacher moves further toward a definition of guardian of faith, "teacher of the Gentiles in faith and truth" (1 Tim. 2:7; cf. 2 Tim. 1:11). The

Pauline understanding of faith as confessional affirmation of the mighty deeds of God has now moved toward understanding of faith as a heritage that the church must guard, both to pass on and to keep pure. We see movement toward what eventually became an understanding of the apostle as guardian of the apostolic tradition (cf. 2 Pet. 3:2), where apostles mediate the commandment of the Lord.

Schuyler Brown best indicates what is happening in Luke and in the whole early church tradition toward the apostles when he observes, "The identification of the apostles with the twelve bears witness to a concern to root the activity of the church in the ministry and intention of Jesus, at a time when the first generation of Christian missionaries was passing from the scene."[33]

Evangelist

The word *evangelist* occurs in the listing of church leaders in Ephesians (4:11). Evangelists are in the third place, following prophets. Apostles and prophets both seem to reflect foundational and time-honored roles in the church (2:20; 3:5). If witnessing the appearance of the risen Christ is fundamental in apostleship, then the confinement of that term to certain early leaders in the church is understandable. Even more, the honoring of the first generation makes sense with the passage of time.[34] Evangelist is to be the new term for leaders in the church that function similarly to the original apostles. As the title makes clear, evangelists are preachers of the gospel with full authority and power (Acts 8:4, 12-14). *To evangelize* was always the verb used to describe the function of the apostles as preachers of the gospel.

Likewise, Luke, who has limited the title apostle by applying it mainly to the Twelve, calls Philip an evangelist (Acts 21:8). Earlier Philip had been preaching the good news of Jesus (8:26-40), reaching out as an itinerant to the fruitless foreign eunuch. Finally, Timothy is enjoined in the Pastorals, "Do the work of an evangelist" (2 Tim. 4:5). This, too, belongs to the later level of tradition where the role of the apostle is seen to belong to the honored past. Nevertheless, the context of the discussion is the authentic preaching of the Word and the reality is to endure suffering. The memory of the apostle is embodied in the evangelist.

So while these three usages do not allow more than a conjecture, it is likely that evangelist, once assigned to apostles as the communicators of the gospel, describes the role or function of the persons who continue the work The evangelist is the one in the church who carries on the work of the apostles at a time when to call oneself an apostle would seem to be a presumptive equating of oneself with the founding figures of Paul and the Twelve, and hence succumbing to the temptation of claiming superstatus. Such an act would deny the fundamental spirit of Christian leadership.

Conclusions about Apostles

Apostles are persons sent most often by the resurrected Lord but occasionally by the historical Jesus or by the congregations under God. All of these appointments are by God.

Their function is preaching and the content of their news centers on the death and resurrection of Jesus, making him known as the Christ. The goal of such preaching is the creation of communities of faith where the gospel is believed and lived. Apostles are agents in the creation of faithful communities. They are congregation builders.

Their mission, as itinerants, has universal church significance as they bind together congregations that are geographically and theologically diverse through their telling of the universal story of Jesus' death and resurrection. Their mission also includes incorporating persons outside the community into God's faithful people.

Because the work of apostles became honored as community founding, the title of apostle eventually came to refer to the

Twelve and Paul, with the result that the name eventually came to be used to designate the persons who continued the basic work and calling of the apostles. Since the name evangelist means "herald of good news" and continues the function of the apostles' preaching for the sake of creating faithful communities, it is fitting that such a name designates the heirs of the apostles.

The antagonists to the apostles are known as false apostles. Their identity is sometimes difficult to discern. However, false apostles seek self-honor, display proofs of their own power, letters of recommendation (testimonials), and reject the suffering and weakness of a true apostle. Yet Paul does not oppose proclamation of Christ by anyone who calls forth legitimate faith (Phil. 1:15-18).

Apostolic Ministry in the Contemporary Church

Where does the apostolic role lodge in the contemporary church? To say that it is outmoded is to lose the foundational and fundamental ministry of the church and to deny the power and the claim of the Resurrection. First, I would contend that the loss of the office of apostle has led to the loss of the awareness of the dynamic of the gospel as a power and reality that is life-shaping and in which service and the life of the servant preacher are given profound meaning regardless of the outcome. Modern questions of discouragement and futility reflect the loss of the awareness of the gospel as a durable force and power in history. Clarity about the apostolic function of preaching could well keep the centrality of faith alive.

Second, the recovery of the centrality of the Resurrection in Christian faith is, in part, a recovery of apostolic identity. The loss of apostolic identity means the lack of awareness of the energizing power and the consequent authority that comes to a church and those of its ministers who live in the light of the renewal that is the Resurrection. That authority is deeply rooted in knowing the risen Christ as Lord of life.

Third, the fact that the church has neglected this foundational ministry is reflected in the establishment mentality of the modern church. Most detrimental has been the fact that theological study has been consigned to the university and not the church. Consequently, theological study has made Paul a doctrinal theologian, not a missionary of the church. Rational theology put theological debate at the center, and Paul, in his self-identified role as an apostle, was bypassed. Theology ceased to be for the sake of the church—its mission and its life of faith. However, Paul's primary concern in the gospel was to transform life by structuring alternative communities that would reshape society's natural way of bringing persons together and giving them recognition.

Fourth, rationalism that upholds universal or general truth devalues special times, places, commitments, and roles. Rationalism especially has trouble with perceiving special persons, such as apostles, set apart for unique functions of the gospel. To identify special roles and functions in the church counters this tradition. Further, such rationalism views all evangelization as imperialistic. While evangelization can be corrupted, attempting to possess the gift of the gospel without sharing it or seeking to embody it in a new community is a deviant of faith.

Fifth, recovering apostolic identity and ministry as a foundational part of the church's life would put stress on nurturing the tradition. Apostolic ministry includes the will to guard and keep the centrality of the cross and the Resurrection in a world of competitive values, especially of superpower, superarms, and superegos. Without apostolic identity the church is tempted to neglect the cross as a sign of the conflict of the gospel and human purposes and to be enamored with identifying itself with the marks of human success. Apostolic ministry also involves the calling of persons courageously to faith both with the formation of new congregations and the call of the "establishment" to radical renewal. The apostolic preacher stands at the transition between the old and the new community and so participates in the suffering that always occurs on this frontier where the ages clash.

Sixth, recovery of apostolic identity is essential if faith is to become the center of the church's reality and life. It is the loss of apostolic identity that has led some liberal churches to exist either for the sake of "companionship" or "action." Companionship is not an end in the Bible. Communities of faith are created by faithful response to the gospel. Loss of apostolic identity has led other persons and congregations to exist for action's sake. Again, it is faithful responses to the gospel that enable the tough and enduring action that characterizes apostles and that can create the alternative community under God in the face of a resistant old order.

Seventh, the formation of the Pauline corpus and the development of the apostle as a basic part of the canon makes clear how important preserving the apostolic voice was to the early church. The canon has meaning for us not only as the gospel but as clear call to let it speak in a contemporary way to the ongoing issues of church and world.

Finally, there are a number of implications for ministry itself. Apostles are those persons who keep all aware that the gospel is the power that resides beyond self and the church's control. It is the given reality that sustains the church, yet persons or congregations are sometimes tempted to think that the power resides in their own spirituality. Apostles sustain the tradition, the story, and are also responsible for the interpretation of the gospel as a present power that both transforms and gives life to the world. It is the combining of tradition and contemporary relevance that Paul does so well as an apostle. The apostle lives under the authority of the gospel. The congregation is called into being and continues in good standing by the apostle's preaching of the gospel. Both the congregation and the apostle are equal partners under the claim of the gospel. Apostles not only preach but they also assess how the congregation "stands" (a resurrection image) in the gospel. This is a continuing responsibility in serving the Resurrection (cf. 1 Cor. 15:1). The apostle asserts authority against the church when the congregation becomes acculturated or in some other way fails to embody the power that was originally made available to them. This evaluation is an essential function of apostolic authority.

To engage in an apostolic ministry, to be an apostolic church, is basic—first—in the life of the church.

2

Prophets

This chapter will explore the meaning and function of prophecy in the New Testament. As with the apostles, we will seek to uncover the literary deposits of the prophets as well as survey the comments about them. The thesis is that the apostles were preachers and bearers of the kerygma (tradition of faith) of the historic saving acts in Christ with the purpose of bringing forth faith. The prophets were persons called to see through a revelation given to them by the power of the Spirit what God is doing in the present in order that people might discern the new times and authority in the presence of the old and so live by hope in the new age that God is inaugurating. Prophets make the reign of God, hidden in the present, manifest so that people might live in a new order.

Prophecy in the New Testament

While the form of the materials differs greatly, there are references to prophets, descriptions of the function of prophets, and most important, the literary product of the work of the prophets scattered throughout the New Testament. Observation of these varied materials as they occur throughout the New Testament will give us a clue to the early church's understanding of the function of the prophets.

Prophets in the Pauline Writings

Paul gives the most thorough discussion of prophets in 1 Corinthians 14, but there are other references to prophets on which we can also draw. The most complete literary deposit that claims to be written by a prophet is the Revelation of John. That work can be tested against the Pauline description. Additional prophetic materials will need to be determined by form and function.

Several characteristics of prophets are clearly revealed in 1 Corinthians 14.[1] While the list of church leaders and functions is extensive in 1 Cor. 12:28, 1 Corinthians 14 focuses on speakers in tongues and prophets. It seems to be these two functions and roles that the Corinthians were confusing and which Paul needed to clarify. The distinction between the two is the polemical issue at stake. Paul has not set out to tell us what prophets are in some general discussion, but we do find out much about prophets as he seeks to clarify the issue at stake. From the discussion we discern the following characteristics of prophets in the early church.

Prophecy must be understood in relation to community. It is a gift bestowed on individual members of the church, but all gifts are to be used for the common good (1 Cor. 12:7). When Paul contrasts speaking in tongues with prophecy (14:5), prophecy is chosen because it is the highest of the gifts listed that is characteristic of the local church and its life. Prophecy is desirable, not because it is more spiritual, but because it builds up the church (14:3, 4, 12); when speaking in tongues the believer only edifies self.[2] If one is speaking to God, no one understands unless there is an interpreter present; prophecy speaks to people for building up the church. It is summed up,

"Those who prophesy speak to other people for their upbuilding and encouragement and consolation [*oikodome, paraklesis, paramuthia*]" (14:3). The words *build up* and *encourage* or *exhort* reveal the purpose of prophecy. This refrain resounds through the rest of chapter 14: "Since you are eager for spiritual gifts, strive to excel in them for building up the church" (12), or as finally summed up, "Let all things be done for building up" (26).

Prophecy is preferred over tongues in local worship because it meets the mark by which the whole church is measured. Love builds up while knowledge puffs up (1 Cor. 8:1, cf. 10:23). Each person is not to please self but is rather to edify neighbors (Rom. 15:2; cf. 14:19). Paul's exercise of authority in his conflict with Corinth has been given him "for building you up and not for tearing you down" (2 Cor. 10:8; cf. also 12:19; 13:10). Like all spiritual gifts, it must serve the common good (1 Cor. 12:7).

Yet prophecy is more specific in function. It does not build in general, but it builds up the congregation specifically by encouragement and consolation (1 Cor. 14:3). Prophecy is the sign to believers that God comes to them. For outsiders or unbelievers prophecy, when heard, means conviction, a call to new accountability, discerning the secrets of one's heart, and repentant worship, declaring, "God is really among you" (14:25).

The same two words together in 1 Thess. 2:12, translated *urging and encouraging*, describe Paul and his co-workers' presence with the congregation, calling them to "lead a life worthy of God, who calls you into his own kingdom and glory" (cf. Phil. 2:1). In 2 Cor. 5:20, God appeals (from *paraclesis*) through us (the believers) to "be reconciled to God." Prophetic preaching in the congregation calls persons or recalls believers to the new life worthy of the Lord, confronting them with their own identity. While the word *hope* is not used, hope is conveyed through the prophetic vocation of exhortation and encouragement, calling persons to the total purpose of God.

Specifically, prophecy is primarily part of the public worship of the local congregation. Pursuing love and desiring spiritual gifts in Corinth in the context of worship means "especially that you may prophesy" (1 Cor. 14:1). This primacy of prophecy in local worship is reiterated (14:5) and repeats in the climax, "Be eager to prophesy" (14:39).[3] Paul evidently does not expect all Christians to be prophets and to prophesy, but he does exhort all those with the gift of the Spirit for inspired speech to prophesy rather than speak in tongues. In local worship, prophecy is the expression of love as discussed in 1 Corinthians 13. This is made clear in two ways: by the application of pursuing love to prophesy (14:1) and by the stress on prophecy to build up the church (love builds up). Prophecy is love in action in the setting of worship in Corinth.

Prophecy is equal to tongues and other local church manifestations only in one way. Prophecy, tongues, and knowledge all pass away (1 Cor. 13:8-12; cf. 13:1-3). None is ultimate. It is not prophecy that abides but only the love that is embodied in it (13:13). Prophecy, too, is a gift from God, and not a claim upon God.

Prophecy gives *revelation*. This is implied in the form: "How will I benefit you unless I speak to you in some revelation or knowledge or prophecy or teaching?" (1 Cor. 14:6). So revelation comes from prophecy, knowledge from teaching. This is clarified in the discussion of how prophets function: "Let two or three prophets speak, and let the others weigh what is said. If a revelation is made to someone else sitting nearby, let the first person be silent. For you can all prophesy one by one, so that all may learn [*manthano*] and all be encouraged [*parakaleo*]" (14:29-31). The revelations given to the prophets at Corinth came within the context of a local worshipping community. That is the setting in which God gives authoritative revelation.[4]

Implicit in bringing a revelation is the stress on public proclamation. Prophecy as bringing a revelation demands that the revelation be publicly set forth and not privately appropriated, as was fitting for speaking in tongues. Prophecy again contrasts with tongue-speaking, since the tongue-speaker speaks "mysteries in the Spirit," not revelations. "Nobody understands them" (1 Cor. 14:2). Prophecy reveals the mystery.[5] Other passages in Paul indicate a similar understanding of prophecy: "according to the revelation of the mystery that was kept secret for long ages but is now disclosed, and through the prophetic writings is made known to all the Gentiles, according to the command of the eternal God" (Rom. 16:25-26; cf. 1 Cor. 15:51; Rom. 11:25f.; Eph. 3:3-5; Matt. 10:26; Luke 12:2). While the mystery that prophecy discloses is primarily in the present, Paul also uses revelation in an eschatological context (Rom. 6:18).[6]

The authority for the revelation of prophetic speech is the Spirit of God. The prophet is open to the present work of the Spirit. This is reflected in "Do not quench the Spirit. Do not despise the words of prophets" (1 Thess. 5:19-20). Any Christian, in the occasion of public worship, might become an agent of the Spirit and prophesy (1 Cor. 14:24-25, 30-32). Prophetic leaders have authority only as their speech is recognized as inspired by God and therefore an expression of the will of God.[7]

That the Spirit is the builder of community fits with prophecy as a community function since the authority for revelation is the Spirit of God. The local situation seems to reflect the assumption that the Spirit speaks in an ordered way in the community. When the Spirit speaks to another, the first is to keep silent. This assumes that the Spirit is finished speaking to the first person when the second begins. The Spirit supports speaking one by one for the community's edification. Grudem points out that Paul assumes that the prophet can "control" the emotions so that prophecy in the congregation is always ordered.[8]

Yet we must remember that the mystery the prophet discloses is always surprising and incomprehensible in an age centered in human control and management. For what is disclosed is God's surprising rule where human calculation and control do not operate and where a new power center confounds the established structures. Because of this, the wisdom of God always appears as folly to the old order; conversely, that which the rulers of this age call wisdom is rendered folly (cf. 1 Cor. 1:26-2:13). Paul describes the prophetic function of the community as "We speak God's wisdom, secret and hidden . . . revealed to us through the Spirit," or "We speak of these things in words not taught by human wisdom but taught by the Spirit" (2:7,10,13). Yet a community in the Spirit is necessary to hear these revelations of the new age (1 Cor. 2:13-16).

The knowledge that the prophet imparts is only a glimpse of the new age, never the whole reality. Prophecy is "in part" and its knowledge is "in part." It will pass away even as all else that belongs to this age passes away. The prophet gives a vision but does not possess nor control the reality toward which the prophet points.

The congregation is called to weigh (discern or distinguish, *diakrino*) what is said.[9] This accounts for the related pair of terms in the listing of the gifts: "to another prophecy, to another the discernment of spirits" (1 Cor. 12:10). Prophecy is not an individual phenomenon, nor is the prophet elevated above the community. The prophet claims a revelation of the Spirit, but other prophets and community members weigh (discern) what is said (14:29). Discerning the Spirit is as crucial as prophecy itself. Prophets can be deceived by lying spirits. The function of discerning and testing the spirits belong to other prophets—"The spirits of prophets are subject to the prophets" (14:32) but is also shared by the whole congregation, since all can prophesy (1 Cor. 14:31). Failure to "discern" seems to be a peculiar problem at Corinth.[10]

Here again we see the communal dimension of prophecy in that what prophets say may be individually slanted or misconstrued, so the Spirit in the community evaluates and discerns what is good in what the prophets say.[11] The Spirit is in dynamic dialog between the speaking prophets and the hearing community. This leads to a tremendous confidence in the Spirit-filled quality of life when the edifying prophets speak under the Spirit and the community hears under the Spirit.

Elsewhere, Paul uses this same combination: "Do not quench the Spirit. Do not despise the words of prophets, but test everything" (1 Thess. 5:19-20). Prophecy, under the ruse of spirituality, can be easily abused. Since the gift of the Spirit belongs to the whole community, it must discern whether any specific revelation is the divine will or the prophet's individual idiosyncrasy. False prophets live for themselves and are not under the authority of the Spirit in community. The temptation of prophecy is individualism, which is destructive to the theological basis of the community, "for God is a God not of disorder but of peace" (1 Cor. 14:33). "God of peace" is a liturgical confession that is deeply imbedded in the worship life of the community (cf. Rom. 15:33; 16:20; 2 Cor. 13:11; Phil. 4:9; 1 Thess. 5:23). It means finally that worship must be done in graceful order (1 Cor. 14:40). Unfortunately, in Corinth the antithesis seems to have been the rule—individualistic expression stressing private experiences.

The conclusion, "for God is a God not of disorder but of peace," further suggests that the spirits of the prophets are God given and therefore subject to God.[12] These spirits build community and so are tested in community. Even in that community there is the further test: "No one speaking by the Spirit of God ever says, 'Let Jesus be cursed!' and no one can say 'Jesus is Lord' except by the Holy Spirit" (1 Cor. 12:3).

That prophets are revealers of the hidden purpose of God is made clear by one of the major uses of the Old Testament. The prophets are quoted as interpreters of current events, including the difficult understanding of the cross (cf. Luke 24:25-27). The Old Testament prophets are revealers of the reality of God's new age. The New Testament community listens to the words of scripture to understand the meaning of the times. The prophets of old continue to speak so that the ways of God can be discerned in the new present. The Spirit continues to speak through them (Acts 1:16; 4:25; 28:25).[13]

Prophecy and the Revelation of John

There is a large work, clearly identified as written by the prophet John, by which we can test these characteristics identified in Paul. Does John's functioning accord and illumine Paul's description?

Paul's description of prophets suggests that their basic efforts are not literary. John must write because of his exile (cf. Jer. 36:4-6). First, John calls his work a revelation (Rev. 1:1; cf. 11:7, 8-12 where he shows "his servants what must soon take place," which is his description of revelation). He is seeking to disclose the mysteries of God underlying the question, "What is God doing in a world where the church suffers death and where evil seems triumphant?" John reveals God's powerful action in such a world. Eschatological hope gives understanding and perspective to what God is now doing. History makes sense, not in its own terms, but when viewed by the prophet in terms of God's coming. John is the interpreter of God's saving action in the present. He is not the usual apocalyptist, waiting for the predetermined future to right the evils of the present, but an interpreter of God's action and purpose in social history, which incorporates those things present and things to come.[14]

The very nature of this revelation uses a form of symbolic communication that makes no sense in the old world but makes powerful sense to a community of faith where God makes all things new. There is no rational explanation of why the good suffer, yet there is a powerful communication here of the meaning of suffering by means of a new language.

John's purpose in this revelation is to bring encouragement and strength to the beleaguered churches. He seeks to build them up in the midst of strife and suffering when it would be easy for them to fall apart. As the New Testament recognizes the fate of prophets in persecution and death (Matt. 23:31; Luke 6:23; 11:47-48; 13:33-34), so John knows that a community already living under the authority of the new age experiences extreme tension with the old (see especially Revelation 13). Living by the reality of hope creates conflict and martyrdom. The specific form of Revelation 2 and 3 includes both encouragement and the call to repentance.[15]

The prophet speaks with authority within the congregation. God authorizes the words and they come with prophetic claim: "Write this, for these words are trustworthy and true" (Rev. 21:5; 22:6). Readers are not to modify or subtract anything from the prophetic word (22:18-19).

The author, while speaking authoritatively, is clearly aware of the danger of putting a false evaluation on his words. In receiving the revelation he describes himself as succumbing to confusion by worshipping the messenger who came to him. Twice, the messenger reproves him: "You must not do that! I am a fellow servant with you and your comrades the prophets" (Rev. 22:9), and "I am a fellow servant with you and your comrades who hold the testimony of Jesus. Worship God! For the testimony of Jesus is the Spirit of prophecy" (19:10; cf. 1 Cor. 12:3).

His commission is to "witness" to the Word of God and the testimony of Jesus, even to all that he saw. But the testimony of Jesus he bears is the same commission given to the whole church, whose martyrs have been slain for the Word of God and the witness they have borne (Rev. 6:9; cf. 20:4; 1 Cor. 12:3 is reechoed here). The prophet's task and the prophetic functioning of the church interplay. The prophet acts within the community that has a prophetic character.

Central to John's prophetic functioning is the inspiration of the Spirit. In describing his task he says, "I was in the Spirit on the Lord's day" (Rev. 1:10), "at once I was in the Spirit" (4:2), and "he carried me away in the Spirit" (17:3). Through the things that the prophet is commanded to write, the Spirit speaks to the churches in a fixed call formula: "Let anyone who has an ear listen to what the Spirit is saying to the churches" (chap. 2-3).[16] The Spirit is the speaker. The prophet stands in the presence of the council of God (cf. Jer. 23:18). This guiding Spirit gives the work its strong tone of prophetic compulsion (Rev. 22:18-19; cf. 1 Cor. 14:37). Prophets must speak. Conversely, the Christian prophet identifies false prophets (Rev. 19:20; 20:10) who lead persons to false worship (13:11-17).

Finally, note how deeply John is rooted in the life of the worshipping community. In this he parallels 1 Corinthians spectacularly.[17] John is separated from seven congregations with whom he has prophetic relationships, yet there is a special group of prophets in the congregations identified alongside the saints and "those who fear thy name" (Rev. 11:16; 16:6; 18:24). The work was written to be read aloud at public worship (1:3). The prophet's experience in the Spirit came on the Lord's Day; by implication the prophet receives the revelation at the time the people from whom he is exiled are gathered in worship. Liturgical hymns, symbols, and themes abound in this work, more than in any other New Testament writing, additionally lending credence to a setting within congregational worship and giving the work its power. The prophet stresses that God is the ultimate object of worship (even as he humorously makes clear that we are inclined to worship the one who brings the message—19:9; 22:8-9). The emphasis on the communication of the Spirit to the churches indicates that the Spirit finds locus both in the prophet and the congregation—prophecy is new speech communicating the Spirit's new age. The prophet draws on the prophetic tradition of the Old Testament as the work of the Spirit but interprets the tradition in the light of Jesus Christ; he roots his work in Old Testament images but he does not quote but transforms all in the light of Jesus Christ.

We have sought to understand prophecy as described in 1 Corinthians 12 through 14 and as reflected in the work written by the prophet John. While the literary technique is different, the Revelation of John exhibits the clear marks of a literary deposit with prophetic identity.

Especially at one point the Gospel of John is clearly identified with the prophetic tradition, perhaps indicating that the Johannine literature comes out of a developing community where Christian prophets had a crucial role. When the gospel gives the Holy Spirit a personal name, it is the *Paraclete*, the Encourager. This ties very closely with Paul's identification of the function of prophecy as encouragement (*paraclesis*). Boring points out further, "Every verb describing the ministry of the Paraclete is directly related to his speech function."[18] The Paraclete has the claim of direct revelation, even as do the prophets, mediating the word of the exalted Christ and perhaps also being the power at work in the Christian prophets of the Johannine community. Notice the function of the Paraclete: the Paraclete will make present all the things that the historical Jesus said, always making the revelation present. This is exactly the prophetic function (John 14:26; 15:26), yet that revelation from God remains hidden to those who live only in this world. "The world cannot receive [the Paraclete], because it neither sees him nor knows him. You know him, because he abides with you, and he will be in you" (14:17). The Johannine Christology pictures Jesus as a prophet like Moses, and the Paraclete continues those prophetic functions in the church through conviction, righteousness, and judgment (16:8-11; cf. 1 Cor. 14:24-25), speaking in Jesus' name, and offering encouragement and exhortation.

Prophets in Luke-Acts

Prophets in the New Testament received revelations from the Spirit of God that helped to uncover realities that are hidden in the present age. So prophets in Luke reveal the meaning of the birth of Jesus. Zechariah is filled with the Holy Spirit and prophesies the meaning of the birth of John (Luke 1:67-79). Similarly, the prophet Simeon, under the Holy Spirit, discloses that the salvation of God for all people has come (2:25-35), and the prophetess Anna gives thanks for the redemption of Jerusalem (2:36-38). The identification of Spirit and prophecy are most completely indicated in the prophet John, who is "in the

Spirit and power of Elijah" (1:15-17 RSV). In Luke the Spirit, through prophecy, looks forward to the new age being realized (cf. 4:17-18).

In Luke Jesus himself is filled with the Spirit (4:1, 14, 18); he speaks of himself as a prophet (4:24)[19] and identifies himself with Elijah and Elisha (4:25-30). The power of Jesus lies in his possession of the Spirit (11:20) and following the defeat of demons, he "rejoiced in the Holy Spirit" (10:17-21; cf. Acts 10:38). It is not surprising that Luke, in passages unique to Luke, stresses the role of Jesus as prophet: "A great prophet has risen among us! . . . God has looked favorably on his people!" (7:16; cf. 1:76; 24:19).[20] Above all, the public ministry of Jesus is introduced with a programmatic prophetic speech (4:16-21).

Jesus sees himself as a prophet insofar as he is destined to share the fate of the prophets (Luke 13:33-35). This prophetic fate, according to Luke, was foreshadowed in Jesus' rejection at Nazareth when he gave the programmatic sermon under the power of the Holy Spirit. The eschatological character of Jesus' speech announcing the new age and calling for response to it is characteristic of the language of Jesus in all the Gospels. In Jesus the age of the Spirit is breaking in, beginning with his baptism and culminating in the Resurrection.

Central to the prophetic activity in the Spirit, as in Paul, is the creation or building up of a new community. So John the Baptist in baptism creates a new people of hope who live already in the light of the Coming One (Luke 3:15-17). It is a community of preparation—a new people—that threatens the foundation of the old community. From these stones God can raise up new children of Abraham (Luke 3:8). Likewise in Acts, Jesus bestows the Spirit that creates the church saying, "You will receive power when the Holy Spirit has come upon you" (Acts 1:8; cf. Luke 24:49). Above all, Pentecost becomes that moment of the full creation of new community. The church itself is the gift of the Spirit with its accompanying power. The risen Lord himself is encountered in the Spirit.[21]

Prophecy is understood as a mark of the Spirit and a sign of the new age in the church. In the Pentecost speech Peter interprets the gift of the Spirit by quoting the prophet Joel, "I will pour out my Spirit upon all flesh, and your sons and your daughters shall prophesy." The reference to prophecy is not merely a part of the quotation but the crux of the issue for Luke. This becomes clear when in continuing the quotation—"Even upon my slaves, both men and women, in those days I will pour out my Spirit"—he adds significantly to Joel's words, "and they shall prophesy" (Acts 2:17-18). By repeating this phrase when it is not in the text, he reveals where the thrust of the passage is for him. Not only is the gift of the Spirit linked to prophecy (cf. 2 Pet. 1:20-21), but prophecy, as in Revelation, is linked to the new age. Prophecy is God's gift to the church, and this gift is the indication that the new age of the Spirit with its own gifts has already begun. As apostles deal primarily with the faith in the remembered acts of God in the Christ event, prophets *look to the new age* and are *agents of hope.*

In Luke, as in Paul and Revelation, prophecy is a communal function and a sign of the new age. In fact, prophets can see the signs of the new age already in the present (for example, the signs in the Gospel of John). The communal dimension is vividly portrayed in action when Paul and Barnabas are commissioned for the first mission to the Gentiles (Acts 13:1-3). The community is at worship. After the Holy Spirit speaks through the prophets and the teachers (the local leaders), hands are laid on Paul and Barnabas. Prophets and teachers are prominent in the worship of the local congregation, and they are vehicles of the Holy Spirit. In this experience the church is called to new action. Prophets and teachers have the specific function of identifying those in the community who have gifts of the Spirit for a specific task. In the Pastorals prophets alone exercise this function (1 Tim. 1:18; 4:14). Persons in the community need help in recognizing the gifts that are theirs. Prophets are the local leaders who can discern the gifts of the Spirit and call persons to respond to them.

Likewise, when those who were baptized into John's baptism confessed that they had never heard that there was a Holy Spirit, Paul laid hands upon them and the Holy Spirit fell upon them. At that point they participated in the speaking in tongues and prophecy (Acts 19:6). Acts identifies both tongues and prophecy as marks of the Spirit without seeking in any way to depreciate tongues in the listing of the gifts of the Spirit.[22] Speaking in tongues is a sign of the Spirit in baptism (10:46).

At Pentecost, "all of them were filled with the Holy Spirit and began to speak in other languages, as the Spirit gave them ability" (Acts 2:4). Luke gives speaking in tongues a special interpretation. It is the fulfillment of the Jewish Pentecost tradition when God offered the law to all nations on that day. Spirit again means receiving a new language—one in whose utterance there is power. The new age means a new, powerful speech. Not only do all the people hear the gospel in their own language on Pentecost with amazing results, but also on another occasion Paul, in the power of the Holy Spirit, blinds the false prophet with scorching condemnation. The Spirit is also responsible for the speech of the disciples in witnessing to their faith with overwhelming boldness (4:8; 13:9-10) and irresistible power (6:10; 18:25-26, 28). The gift of the Spirit means powerful new speech. Nowhere is this new speech more clearly indicated than in the trial of persecution for which there can be no advance preparation. In persecution one learns to live by trust in the Holy Spirit. "When they bring you before the synagogues, the rulers, and the authorities, do not worry about how you are to defend yourselves or what you are to say; for the Holy Spirit will teach you at that very hour what you ought to say" (Luke 12:11-12).[23]

Acts designates a number of persons as prophets and describes the work of several other prophets. Their functioning generally accords with what we have observed elsewhere. Judas and Silas, themselves prophets, exhorted (*parakaleo*) the brethren and strengthened (*episterizo*) them (15:32). While this last word is new in our discussion, it relates closely to *build up* (*oikodomeo*) and takes its place.[24] These two prophets were given the additional role of being emissaries from one congregation to another, designated for this task by the apostles and elders and the church at Jerusalem (15:23). As emissaries, Judas and Silas are to confirm what was written to the church (15:27). They seem to function much as the signature does in the modern letter, authenticating and personalizing its contents. What they specifically authenticate, however, is that the Holy Spirit is really speaking to the hearers through the Jerusalem community: "For it has seemed good to the Holy Spirit and to us" (15:28). Here again the prophets discern the Spirit in the church and encourage (*parakaleo*) and strengthen (*episterizo*) it in the midst of confusion (15:32, 34).[25]

The decision of the Jerusalem Council is under the prophetic authority of discerning the Spirit in the community (cf. 1 Cor. 14:32, 37; 1 Thess. 5:19-21). The Holy Spirit enables the church to deal both with its division and its new reality in a communal way. Further, the events that are happening, the acceptance of the gospel by the Gentiles, must accord with the traditional prophetic insight into the working of God (Acts 15:15-18; cf. Eph. 3:3-6) so that Old Testament prophecy is also used as a means for discerning the Spirit in the community.

The prophet Agabus (Acts 11:28) first appears as an emissary from Jerusalem to Antioch who through the Spirit reveals a famine and thus enables the church to decide on a course of action that meets the crisis responsibly. He is calling the community to accountability on a social issue. His presence later at Caesarea, along with the four daughters of Philip who prophesy (21:9-10), appears more detached. In many ways he resembles a number of Old Testament prophets with his symbolic action and with the introduction of his message with an adapted form of the traditional messenger formula, "Thus says the Holy Spirit," as compared with the Old Testament form, "Thus says Yahweh." He gives a definite revelation. There is no indication here that he is a congregational representative. Different from all others, he appears to be an isolated individual, separated from congregational functioning, who gives oracles. Still, Agabus speaks under the authority of the Holy Spirit, uttering God's word of warning, which is not meant to deter Paul, however. It is not an absolute word. It is to enable him to consciously fulfill his mission by going to Jerusalem in courageous trust (cf. Luke 12:11-12) after the pattern and manner of his Lord. The prophet clarifies and discerns the gift to which another is called; this is a fundamental prophetic function.

Prophecy in Other New Testament Writings

When we move beyond Luke-Acts to the other gospel writers, prophet is not a title that they use of Jesus, nor do they report it as used by the disciples. While they report Jesus' saying, "Prophets are not without honor, except in their hometown" (Mark 6:4), it is only Luke who develops this to require an understanding of Jesus as a prophet. The other Gospels seem to describe people using the term prophet of Jesus before they have come to full faith. So, in John, the Samaritan woman calls Jesus a prophet (4:19), but she is still early in her pilgrimage to understand Jesus. Her climactic confession in the narrative is "Savior of the world" (4:42). Similarly, the man born blind confesses, "He is a prophet" (9:17), when forced by the Pharisees to make some statement. Under their continual persistence and his further encounter with Jesus he confesses, "Lord, I believe," and worships him (9:38).[26]

Matthew does not portray the faith development of persons Jesus encounters as John does. Yet the crowd at the triumphal entry gives the title of prophet to Jesus (Matt. 21:11). The same acclamation by the crowd is the reason for the difficulty of his arrest (21:46). That this estimation is not adequate is clear later in the Passion Story when the crowd denounces him. That prophets get killed is an old story that works no new or great things, only confirms guilt (cf. Mark 6:15; Matt. 23:29-37). Such estimations have been foreshadowed in the response of the disciples to Jesus' question, "Who do people say that the Son of Man is?" (Matt. 16:13). They report that some say Elijah, and others say one of the prophets (16:14). Yet that, too, is an incomplete answer, for Jesus presses them further, "Who do you say that I am?" (16:15).[27]

While prophet is an inadequate word to communicate who Jesus is, Matthew's church has prophets as leaders (23:34) along with the wise. The parallel of "prophets and wise" here with "prophets and righteous" has led Hill to see two groups functioning in Matthew's congregations: prophets and teachers (the righteous).[28] They are the local leaders here as well as in Acts (13:1).

The pastoral Epistles in their description of the functioning of the Christian community reinforce the picture of the prophets' communal function as seen in Acts, in Johannine literature, and in Paul. In the Pastorals, the venerated, elder, apostle Paul is giving charge to his young successors much like the aging seminary professor sends the class into the field with blessing and wisdom. The new generation is not to "neglect the gift [*charismata*] that is in you, which was given to you through prophecy with the laying on of hands by the council of elders" (1 Tim. 4:14, cf. 1:18). The commissioning of the young leader has been sealed both by prophetic speech and the laying on of the hands of the elders.

Evidently, the prophets discerned the presence of the Spirit at work in the church in this act performed by its representative leaders. There would seem to be no basic distinction between whether the congregation or the elders, as congregational representatives, laid on the hands. Here form and Spirit interrelate as the one authenticates and disciplines the other. The gift of the Spirit is communicated and discerned by the prophet in the midst of the congregation. Prophecy is God's gift to the church for its own life and leadership, and the gift of prophecy is one indication that the new age of the Spirit with its gifts (*charismata*) has already begun. These prophetic utterances in the community, which pointed to him for his special task, sustain Timothy in the face of hostility and persecution—that by them he might "fight the good fight" (1 Tim. 6:12).[29]

It is significant that our common view of heroic prophetic individuals seems to be borne out, at most, by one isolated and brief reference—to Agabus. Elsewhere, prophecy is intimately related to the life of a community and speaks to and out of its situation. The Spirit in community, partly through the prophets, sets apart persons for necessary tasks and the prophets in turn test the authenticity of the community's life. So the church can meet famine where it occurs and Timothy can meet conflict and hostility in his own ministry.

A Comparison of Prophets and Apostles

We can compare apostles and prophets in these ways, realizing the functions in persons overlap more than is immediately evident when we attempt to delineate what the fundamental issues are in each calling. For example, Paul does some teaching and prophetic activity even though his basic identity was that of an apostle, and likewise with the others. Even more, setting persons aside for a particular function never means the denial of the function in the wider life and experience of the community. Only functions that are legitimate for the community as a whole merit designation of special persons with special responsibilities for the task.

Apostle	*Prophet*
Itinerant leader (ecumenical)	Local leader
Carries the gospel (the faith or kerygma)	Receives revelations in the Spirit
A preacher or proclaimer	A seer—what God is doing today "watchers and prayers"

| Creates new communities | Enables congregations to discern meaning and keep alive to God's will |
| Calls forth faith | Signs of new age shown in new life (an awake people) |

The prophet is seeking to give a persecuted community a *hope* that lies in seeing just what God is doing in the present, which by contemporary values makes no sense at all. To discern the meaning of the present, all must be seen from the perspective of God's final or eschatological purpose for society. How, in the midst of the realities of suffering, can the community of faith make sense out of and discern the signs of presence and coming of God's new Jerusalem where all dwell together in community? To do so is the fundamental task of the prophet. If the church is a new community, called to live by God's new act of the Resurrection, which initiates the new age, then the prophet is the community leader who discerns the *power and presence of the risen Christ*. Only this will keep the community from losing its hope and vision when it is in tension with the old communities and power structures. The church as a community is always tempted to forget the reality of the reign that is coming (and already is) and to take on the protective coloration of the society around it.

The apostles, by preaching the death and resurrection of Jesus, make clear that the old order, with its values, has given way to a new one. This has occured already in the decisive events surrounding Jesus of history. The prophet is the person who can discern these secular forces as well as God's Spirit in the present as these two ages live in conflict and offer decisive choices to humans. The prophet can distinguish between the wisdom of this age and the wisdom that comes from God (1 Cor. 1:26-31). The prophet sees this tension between God's action and the present and enables the congregation to see all the signs of the new in its midst. The prophetic community lives out of the reality of the Resurrection. No wonder Paul can say, "First apostles, second prophets" (1 Cor. 12:28). Apostles create the new community; prophets maintain the vision by which it can live.

Watch and Pray

Now the question is, can we find the way(s) indirectly disclosed in the New Testament that would show the prophets helping the community discern the power and the presence of God in the midst of the historical ambiguities of life? Are there words, phrases, or images that reflect prophetic activity at work? Can we identify places where prophets call persons to discern the new in the midst of the old order and where they see the possibility of living by God's new reality?

The imagery in the New Testament is rich and varied. The words *to rise (resurrection)* literally mean *to awake* from sleep, even the sleep of death. If the church is to be a community of the new age, a resurrection community, it must "be awake," not sleeping. Most vividly then the words *to rise from the dead* and *to watch* are from the same etymological root. They are interrelated in form as well as in image. This is beautifully expressed in the congregational hymn recorded in Eph. 5:13: "Sleeper, awake! / Rise from the dead, / and Christ will shine on you." The church is to be that watchful, awake community that lives, not in obscurity, but in the enlightenment of the gospel. This image of new life, in which the enlightenment of the gospel contrasts with the obscurity of death, sleep, and night, receives elaboration in a rich symphonic way. So the prophet John exhorts, "See, I am coming like a thief! Blessed is the one who stays awake and is clothed, not going about naked and exposed to shame" (Rev. 16:15) Woe to the church that is not awake, living the gospel, walking in the light.

God's coming is always surprising, unannounced, like that of a thief in the night. Such a coming is no threat to the one who is awake, because the wakeful person is dressed, wearing the garments of the gospel, or as expressed in ethical passages elsewhere, has "put on the Lord Jesus Christ" (Rom. 13:14, Gal. 3:27).

The person who is not awake, not living the life of the new age, is asleep and is caught naked, living in the night when one is undressed and therefore has not put on the new lifestyle. To such a person the coming of Christ will indeed be a robbery (cf. Rev. 3:3-5; 19:8).

This rich and elaborate metaphor receives even larger development in the familiar passage in 1 Thess. 5:1-11. In addition to being people of the new community, being awake means to be sound or sober—responsible—in one's actions. Drunkenness—irresponsibility—also occurs in the image at night when one is not living the resurrection life. So faith, love, and hope (5:8) characterize the wakeful life of the resurrection community. Lest we be overwhelmed with always being "awake," remember, to be "in Christ" is to be a child of the new age and, therefore, watchful or awake, whether we are literally awake or sleeping (5:10).

This prophetic image of the community also leads us into the heart of the gospel. Mark uses "watch and pray" in only two passages. He reports it in Jesus' parable that ends the thirteenth chapter, Jesus' last teaching. The Passion Story, Crucifixion, and Resurrection follow. It is as if this parable of the master who went on a journey is to help us understand the great events that follow—the heart of the gospel. It literally tells us, the readers as well as the disciples, "to watch."[30] It begins, "Beware, keep alert; for you do not know when the time will come." It ends, "And what I say to you I say to all: Keep awake" (Mark 13:33, 37). The issue is absolutely clear. The master in the parable may come in the evening, at midnight, at cockcrow, in the morning.

That is a recital of the decisive hours in the passion story that follows: the evening—the Lord's Supper with the disciples' pride; midnight—sleeping in the garden and the arrest; cock-crow—the denial; morning—the crucifixion where the disciples flee. At every point in the narrative that follows, the disciples either literally or figuratively sleep—while God is coming and doing mighty and decisive acts. Readers are likewise tempted to sleep. This is written to a church that is not wakeful and that is missing, therefore, the works that God is actively performing.

The other place Mark uses this imagery is the Gethsemane story that follows (14:32-42). The disciples are commanded to keep awake. When Jesus returns he finds them sleeping. "Simon, are you asleep? Could you not keep awake one hour? Keep awake and pray that you may not come into the time of trial; the spirit indeed is willing, but the flesh is weak." Notice that to sleep is to enter temptation, to stumble and fall, as Peter does in the denial. Three times the disciples fail to watch and pray, and so they sleep. No wonder they cannot see what God is doing on the cross. As children of this age it is defeat for them—folly; therefore, no wonder that they stumble and fall.[31]

In the whole process Jesus is the watchful one, who is awake and who can see that God is at work in a surprising way. Jesus is able to see and watch, because he is the one who prays in Gethsemane. Prayer, being in relationship to God, is the only possibility for seeing with new eyes. Watching is possible only when it is rooted in relationship with God. It demands prayer and openness to the divine leading.

Prayer and prophecy are linked in numerous places, though this sounds surprising to modern ears. So Anna the prophet "never left the temple but worshiped there with fasting and prayer night and day" (Luke 2:37). In Acts it was while the prophets and teachers (and the congregation?) were worshipping and fasting that the Holy Spirit disclosed the special gifts to Paul and Barnabas (13:1-2).

Not only Luke, with his special interest in prayer, but Paul also links prayer and prophesying as joint activities in Corinthian worship (11:4-5), as he does again in Thessalonica.[32] Of course, the whole discussion of 1 Corinthians 14 links prayer (worship) and prophecy. The discussion in verses 13 through 19 is seen as related to the chapter as a whole when it is recognized that prophets are the ones who pray in the community. "I will pray with the spirit, but I will pray with the mind also." The congregation needs to know when to say "Amen" to the thanksgiving, so that they are involved. Speaking in a tongue and prophecy seem to be paralleled here to praying in a tongue, where the Spirit prays and the mind does not (14:14) and praying where the spirit and the mind pray. The latter then must characterize prophecy.[33]

The image is reversed in the stilling of the storm. There Jesus sleeps. Because he trusts God, he does not fear the storm or the threat of evil.[34] The disciples, fearful of the threat to life, cannot sleep for they do not trust God. For them it is the terror of the night. Being awakened, Jesus has the power that rebukes the wind and calms the sea (Mark 4:35-41).[35]

Prophets (and the disciples as the prophetic community) are given what the prophets of old really longed for: "But blessed are your eyes, for they see, and your ears, for they hear. Truly I tell you, many prophets and righteous people longed to see what you see, but did not see it, and to hear what you hear, but did not hear it" (Matt. 13:16-17).

Prophets and Teachers

Separation between functions is never absolute, and since prophets and teachers are both primarily local leaders, they are sometimes mentioned together (Acts 13:1; 1 Cor. 14:6), and their functions seem to overlap. So when encouraging responsible local worship, Paul suddenly includes knowledge (teaching) and then discusses the integration of the mind and the Spirit in the worship of the Corinthian congregation. This focuses most clearly around the term *encouragement*. Encouragement is a function of prophets, but the word recurs often in ethical catechisms shaped by the teaching tradition of the church. This suggests that teaching is seen within the prophetic context of supporting and calling people to live out their faithfulness daily. Teachers bring the prophetic function into everyday life. The boundary between the prophetic interpretation of scripture under the Spirit and the careful teaching of it is blurred in the common task of building up the community of faith. For congregational health both functions must be performed, and they become integrated in the common task of encouragement.[36] Like all those who function, teachers have their charismatic gift, and they, too, exercise authority in their fulfillment of it.

The distinction is that prophets under the authority of the Spirit give a revelation. They are not bound by scripture or tradition. The prophet interprets the faith as it relates to life, as an agent of hope. The teacher seeks to describe that new life as it is now, rooted in the tradition of the teaching of Jesus. As such they are the interpreters of love.

Conclusions about Prophets in the New Testament

Prophets give revelations from God. They not only have a gift of the Spirit so that they can disclose the divine message and will to the community, even more they have the gift to discern the diverse gifts of the Spirit in other members of the congregation who are called to special tasks and they are able to help them respond to their calling.

Prophets function primarily within the local community and, along with the teachers, are the local leaders in worship. Their revelations come within the context of the community's worship of God where an alternative consciousness is being shaped. Here the coming reign can be seen in the midst of a world of social oppression. The prophet's ultimate concern is that we worship the true God since we are shaped by what we worship. The prophets are those who attack idolatry or false worship because it corrupts society.

Prophets and prophetic activity are a sign of the new age of the Spirit and its presence within the church. Therefore, the prophets are communicators of hope and the discerners of the presence of the Spirit, which is the sign of hope. Further, as persons of the new age, prophets have a new language and a new vision. Only from this perspective can prophets make sense of out that which is experienced as chaotic (as the suffering of the church that forms the setting for the Book of Revelation).

The temptation of false prophecy is always present. It serves false gods that are now visible and often takes the form of mechanical prediction or of clairvoyance. It is not attuned to God's hidden and living presence, which is the basis for ultimate hope.

Prophets are the inheritors of the apostolic tradition. They disclose the future of that tradition and thus both sustain and give vision to the communities of faith in their ongoing life. The community is framed by the apostolic story and called to the vision that story gives for the future.

The Prophetic Church

The prophetic task of ministry is to discern the gifts of God in persons in the congregation. Persons are not always aware of their own gifts, but a prophetic congregation and ministry help persons discover their gifts and use them in an appropriate way. In this way the community is necessary for discerning and testing the spiritual gifts of the members of Christ's body.

Corollary with this recognition of gifts is the need to help parishioners recognize the use of their own gifts as a calling. We need to be delivered from voluntarism and optionalism about the tasks of the congregation. Volunteering implies God has no claim on us. It creates a false view of freedom, as if we could live without any claim upon ourselves. Then when we do volunteer, we experience the syndrome of needing to be thanked for what we have done and are subject to the temptation of self-esteem for doing what we did not have to do. Such a concept of voluntarism may reflect the American understanding of separation of church and state, but it does not do justice to the covenantal claim and calling of God for God's people. It should be clear that the calling of persons to use their gifts can take place only within the whole context of worship where the Spirit rules. The Spirit is basic for a true understanding and testing of the gifts by the community in the light of God's reign and will.

A prophetic ministry will communicate what has been fundamentally lost in the modern church—a sense of God's coming new age. Decisions are not to be made merely in terms of what is possible within the realm of the old age. God will be seen as purposeful and at work in history, though the divine presence is hidden so that prophets are needed to disclose it. The prophetic function sees history under God's rule. Without this vision, the sense of destiny and calling for the whole church is lost.

This function is basically that of instilling hope—calling persons out of their confined worlds where nothing is possible except what already exists. Such a world knows only confinement and limitation; it is a modern enslavement. The calling of a prophetic church is to live by hope rooted in God's new work, not to live by what past conditioning has taught us to recognize as possible.

3

Teachers

The teaching function in the New Testament church was widespread, judging both by the extant teaching materials and by the predominance of certain words like *teach, teacher, teaching, doctrine, learn,* and *disciple.* There is the tradition of Jesus as a teacher and the material known as Q upon which much of Matthew and Luke are based. There are collections of ethical materials in the Gospels like the sermons in Matthew, catechistic materials in the Epistles (Col. 3:1-4:6; Eph. 4:1-6:9; 1 Pet. 2:11-4:7), and the extended ethical materials at the end of the Pauline letters and the Epistle of James.

An examination of these many references to teaching and its function will enlarge our awareness of the nature of its practice and value in the early church. We will then examine some of the teaching documents themselves to discern what can be discovered about the nature of teaching in the early church.

Jesus as Teacher

There are many references in Mark to Jesus as teacher and to his teaching. He teaches in the synagogue (1:21), by the sea

(2:13; 4:1), in the villages (6:6), as do the Twelve (6:30); he teaches his disciples privately (9:31) and in the temple (11:17; 12:35). Marcan tradition shows Jesus as a teacher in many situations, and the disciples address him as teacher (4:38; 9:38; 10:35; 13:1), as do the father of the demented child (9:17), the rich young man (10:17, 20), and a scribe (12:32). He is remembered as a teacher.

Both the verb *to teach* (Matt. 5:2; 7:29) and the noun *teaching* (Matt. 7:28), as well as the more general word *sayings* (Matt. 19:1; 26:1), are used to refer to the collected bodies of Jesus' teaching such as the codified ethical materials in the Sermon on the Mount. Matt. 11:1 applies teaching to a codified presentation of the disciples' mission responsibility. It also refers to understanding the suffering of the Son of Man (Mark 8:31), which is related closely to the understanding of discipleship (8:34-38; 9:31).

The verb to teach in the Hebraic and Greek Septuagint tradition describes the activity of one who communicates the will of God and declares it with its demands. It does not refer to the development of human understanding and potential as is the case in the Hellenistic world.[1] God is ultimately the source of all teaching and of the teacher. The focus is on the divine will and understanding the claim of God on the whole person. Teaching such as "Strive first for the kingdom of God and his righteousness" (Matt. 6:33) roots Jesus deeply in this Hebraic tradition.

Further, in the case of Jesus, the sense of his own relationship with God meant that his teaching is rooted deeply in the claim and being of his own person. This is reflected both in his form of address, "Truly, I tell you" (not even, "Thus says the Lord"), and in the response, "They were astounded at his teaching, for he taught them as one having authority, and not as the scribes. . . . They were all amazed, and they kept on asking one another, 'What is this? A new teaching—with authority!'" (Mark 1:22, 27). The command and the will of God are laid upon the hearers with all the power and authority that consciousness of relationship with God gives. Hence, Jesus' teaching is remembered as qualitatively different in authority from that of the contemporary scribes. By contrast, scribal teaching had become a citing of and holding on to tradition to preserve Judaism from erosion by the attitudes of Hellenistic society around it.

This sense of unique and decisive authority in Jesus' teaching of the will of God, which is fully embodied in his person, accounts for the surprising fact that the disciples are never accorded the title of teacher in the Gospels; they are only preachers of the rule of God and of the Good News. Therefore, they can be called apostles but never teachers in Jesus' presence. They can become witnesses to Jesus, but they cannot become teachers, for gospel teaching is rooted in Jesus' unique identity. In their relation to him, Jesus is always the teacher, they are always disciples—learners. Only when the Twelve return from being sent forth by Jesus is the activity of the disciples described by the verb taught (Mark 6:30). They can teach only when they are under his direct authority and commission. Fundamentally, teaching is a word that describes the activity of Jesus.

The word to learn, from which disciple (learner) comes, has the same Hebrew root as the Hebrew word teach, and therefore the same fundamental meaning. Learning is coming to know God's will and practicing it. God decides on what is to be learned and is the center of learning. To be a disciple is to be in the process of becoming subject to the revealed will of God.[2]

Yet, to learn is only a partial description of discipleship in the Gospels and Acts. The primary description of the role of the disciple is not as a learner but in the verb *to follow*. Following is more characteristic of the function of the disciple than learning, in spite of the meaning of the word disciple itself. This means that learning of Jesus is characterized by submitting to the claim of Jesus, following his person, especially in the way of suffering. This is reflected in Matthew's use of learn: "Take my yoke upon you, and learn from me" (Matt. 11:29). The content of learning has moved from submission to scripture to subjection to the way of Jesus himself. Following Jesus involves the possibility of breaking all other primary ties (Matt. 8:22; Luke 9:61). It means sharing in Jesus' destiny of having no place to lay one's head (Matt. 8:19); it means the possibility of taking up one's cross (Mark 8:34) and being like the Master in being rejected by this generation. Yet following also means to share in the light of God (John 8:12) and in God's redemption of humans (Rev. 14:4) and the blessings of salvation. The fact that there is no noun form, only the verb form, of following essentially suggests how discipleship is an activity.

By contrast, disciple is found only in the Gospels and Acts, occurring some 250 times. Jesus calls disciples, and that is a permanent role in relation to him. It is not something from which one graduates, thereby advancing to master status. Disciples are bound to obey and follow Jesus, thus fulfilling their destiny—always as disciples who hear the word of Jesus. His ultimate and final relation to them is that of Lord. Disciple is the name for Christian in Acts (for example, 6:1; 9:1; 16:1). As disciples they are "obedient to the faith" (6:7), "continue in the faith" (14:22; cf. 18:23, 27 and John 8:31), and "filled with joy and the Holy Spirit" (Acts 13:52).

That discipleship is the fundamental status becomes especially clear in John. Raymond Brown points out that this emphasis corrects any tendency in the New Testament to transform a leadership role into a divine office. While Paul stressed the diversity of gifts in the community, John stresses the fundamental equality of all disciples before Christ. Instead of stressing the diversity of that which grows on the vine, John makes clear that all branches are dependent on the vine (chap. 15).

The unique stress in John is on the disciple that Jesus loved. The love relationship gives meaning to life, and this reality emphasizes personal meaning, not leadership function. As a result, John plays down the leadership roles, lest they be magnified in status before God.[3] The disciple whom Jesus loved communes with him at the Last Supper, is present at the cross and welcomed into the family of Jesus, and believes at the empty tomb. The love relationship is fundamental to discipleship and enables one to share in the new life of the Resurrection, for Lazarus, the one who was raised in the gospel, together with his sisters, are the only ones identified as loved by Jesus.

As Rengstorf points out, John further develops the unique understanding that Jesus' teaching proceeds out of the revelation given to him. Teaching is what Jesus alone can give because of the unique parent-child relation: "I do nothing on my own, but I speak these things as the Father instructed me. And the one who sent me is with me; he has not left me alone, for I always do what is pleasing to him" (8:28-29).[4] Here it is clear that teaching communicates the claim and will of God and that the teacher must be the one who "does" the teaching. In like manner, only the Holy Spirit can disclose the revelation of God, which, indeed, Jesus' teaching is: "But the Advocate, the Holy Spirit, whom the Father will send in my name, will teach you everything, and remind you of all that I have said to you" (John 14:26).[5] The Holy Spirit, sent by Jesus, continues Jesus' teaching in the church (cf. 16:13-14). As teacher, the Holy Spirit is also the Spirit of Truth.

Jesus is the teacher; teaching comes from Jesus. Of the forty-eight uses of teacher in the Gospels, forty-one are applied to Jesus, stressing his unique role as teacher. The word teacher occurs only ten other times in the New Testament, of which only three are in Paul. Similarly, the verb to teach occurs fifty-six times in the Gospels: sixteen times in Acts, nine in Paul (ten with Ephesians), and eleven additional times in the rest of the New Testament.

Implications of Jesus as Teacher

Teacher may seem too humble a title when applied to Jesus, as if he is like everyone else. People who want no Christology assume that it is harmless to call Jesus a teacher. The term is assumed to have a minimal meaning: "I can accept Jesus as a teacher if not in any other way."

Yet teacher is a high title. The role of teacher distinguishes him from the disciples as well as the scribes and everyone else. In Jesus, to be a teacher is related to the claim of God. The title is transformed. It takes on new meaning when used to describe the experience and person of Jesus. The title actually becomes exalted.

In the foot-washing in John, Jesus affirms, "You call me Teacher and Lord—and you are right, for that is what I am. So if I, your Lord and Teacher, have washed your feet..." (13:13-14). Lord and teacher are equally significant titles. Each authorizes the other. Mary calls the risen Lord, "Teacher."

In summary, the following points seem clear: Teaching is communicating the claim of God. In order to do that Jesus associates with all kinds of persons. The claim set forth needs to be embodied in Jesus the teacher in his relation to God. Teaching is not setting forth a body of learning as is the case with the traditional rabbi or teacher. As such, Jesus alone is the teacher in the Gospels. Teacher is a very exalted title. The disciples are always just that—learners, followers. Jesus does not train disciples as successors as did the rabbis and professional teachers. The goal of Jesus' teaching is not the development of a school or of a next generation of teachers. Teaching is an activity carried on by God through the Holy Spirit in the ongoing life of the church. Teaching is predominantly ethical, seeking to awaken responsibility for the life of the rule of God in the human community.

Teaching in the Church Tradition

In Matthew the fundamental transition of teaching in the church is established. The disciples are incorporated into the teaching role by the Resurrection. The risen Christ claims all authority as reigning ruler and commands his followers to disciple the nations. That is accomplished, in part, by "teaching them to obey everthing that I have commanded you." The disciples are now given the role of teachers of the word of Jesus in the ongoing life of the church. Jesus is still the authority, but the disciples are to bear the teaching tradition that has been established by Jesus (Matt. 28:16-20).

Teaching is dangerous since one is tempted to become confused and forget that Jesus is the teacher. We are not apt to think that we are the Messiah, but we may assume that teacher is a lofty title that a church person can claim. We have already observed how reticent Paul is to use the word teacher in spite of the legitimizing of a group of teachers in the church through the Resurrection.

However, the situation in Matthew differs markedly from Mark in the use of the title teacher. Even though Matthew is a teaching gospel with its sermons of collected teaching, Matthew, like us, is inclined to see the title of teacher as limited. While Jesus is continually described as teaching (4:23; 5:2; 7:29; 9:35; 11:1; 13:54; 21:23; 26:55), the disciples do not address Jesus as teacher. He is addressed as teacher by the scribes (8:19; 12:38), Pharisees (9:11; 22:16, 36), tax collectors (17:24), the rich young man (19:16), and the Sadducees (22:24). Never, however, do the disciples address him as teacher.[6] For Matthew, contrary to Mark, teacher clearly is not an adequate title. While Jesus teaches, the appropriate address is something other than teacher, something that clarifies the claim of God through his person and his teaching.[7] Matthew wants to make clear that Jesus brings a divine claim. For Matthew teacher remains a general and secular word.

Yet in describing Jesus' activity, Matthew uses the verb to teach and the noun teaching in specific places. Still the verb occurs less in the longer Gospel of Matthew than it does in Mark, as does the noun.[8] With the great amount of additional teaching material in Matthew and the way it is systematically gathered, this difference is astounding.

Matthew uses teach to introduce the Sermon on the Mount (5:2) and the mission sermon (9:35), as well as to conclude them

(7:29; 11:1). It also occurs twice in the decisive introduction to the main body of the Sermon on the Mount (5:17-20). In addition, teaching is a function that the disciples are to carry on (28:20). When these special uses are recognized,[9] we see that Matthew clearly uses teach in the same ways as Mark only seven times (Mark 1:22, twice; 6:2, 6; 7:7, a Septuagint quote; 12:14; 14:49). Dropped are the uses of the word referring to Jesus' teaching in the temple (Mark 12:35; 11:17) and teaching the crowd (6:34; by the sea in 4:1, 2; 2:13). Matt. 13:53 preserves the Mark 6:2 reference to teaching in the synagogues and relocates the generalized teaching in villages in Mark 6:6 into the synagogue in Matt. 9:35. Twice Matthew substitutes healing for Mark's teaching, evidently finding it a more appropriate action among the crowds (compare Matt. 14:14 and 19:2 with Mark 6:34 and 10:1).

We conclude that for Matthew teaching is a more formal activity, identified as a function in the synagogue and something that introduces a clearly definable and structured content of material. The teaching tradition of the church is being given shape in a more systematic educational approach to life that is appropriately directed to the community of faith. Further, the model of Jesus as teacher is focused on a situation by presenting his teaching in structured sermons that address major issues of concern for the faith community.

Luke parallels Matthew in that Jesus is never addressed as teacher by the disciples in the gospel. In addition, the number of times Jesus is called teacher in direct address by others is increased to twelve times. Teacher is not an adequate title in Luke either. Only those removed from Jesus use it. However, Luke also pictures Jesus' teaching in many kinds of situations. He does not identify teaching with structuring of material or in the synagogue as Matthew does.

In Paul and the rest of the New Testament, the verb to teach and the noun teacher are used infrequently. The noun teacher occurs only three times in Paul. Twice it refers to a church office in the lists in 1 Corinthians (12:28, 29; cf. Eph. 4:11 for the deutero-Pauline use).[10] "To teach" occurs in Rom. 12:7 in the listing of the gifts in the community and describes the function of church leaders. Twice Paul directly describes his own activity as teaching (1 Cor. 4:17; Col. 1:28), and also the ethical code suggests it is an activity within the congregation (Col. 3:16). Teaching is a recognized function in the church and teachers are a specific group.

Significantly, teaching as a noun is used to refer to an inherited and accumulated knowledge passed on in the church (*didache* in Rom. 6:17 and 16:17; cf. 2 Thess. 2:15, "the traditions that you were taught"). In 1 Cor. 4:17 Paul teaches in every church "my ways in Christ." Timothy can bring this teaching to remembrance. Here, too, Paul has an identifiable content of teaching in mind. In Rom. 15:4 the instruction (*didaskalia*) was written in former days; it is an identifiable body of teaching. In Gal. 1:12 Paul rejects being taught the gospel by persons. God is the true teacher and Paul's authority rests in that divine revelation. Nevertheless, here again there is a body of teaching that can be passed on, but such a body may be corrupted (Eph. 4:14; cf. Col. 2:22) or faithful (Rom. 6:17; 16:17; cf. 12:7). Faithful teaching can be identified in form and function as to persons who perform it (1 Cor. 14:6) or in the situation of congregational worship where it occurs (1 Cor. 14:26; cf. Col. 3:16).[11]

We conclude that in Paul, like Matthew, teaching is a clearly defined activity in the church that communicates what it means to live in the ways of Christ. Furthermore, those teachings have meaning only when rooted in the community that bears an ongoing tradition and is a body that gathers in worship.

Again Ephesians, using "teaching" but once, has within it a context that suggests the school of Christ (4:20-21). Colossians continues the hint that teaching is a grounding and a confirming of persons in the faith. "As you therefore have received Christ Jesus the Lord, continue to live your lives in him, rooted and built up in him and established in the faith, just as you were taught, abounding in thanksgiving" (2:6-7). The context of communal worship roots teaching in the faith and gives it the body of a communal tradition (3:16).

The deutero-Pauline tradition makes teaching ability one of the requirements for a bishop (1 Tim. 3:2) or for the Lord's servant (2 Tim. 2:24). It is a gift exercised in public worship (1 Tim. 4:13). The number of references to teaching as an activity and the identification of a body of teaching is greatly multiplied in the pastoral Epistles. The community addressed in Hebrews has not fulfilled the requirement of teaching because of its failure to hear and grow (5:11-14).

The purpose of all teaching is that persons grow into maturity, growing in the knowledge and understanding of the meaning of the faith so that their faculties are trained by practice to distinguish good and evil (Heb. 5:14; 6:1). Or as Ephesians puts it, "Speaking the truth in love, we must grow up in every way into him who is the head, into Christ" (4:15). Such incorporation into Christ means the whole community "makes bodily growth and upbuilds itself in love" (4:16 RSV).[12] Teaching is concerned with community growth in the present as a result of encountering the reality of the gospel; it focuses on the ethical claim of the gospel as it is embodied in obedient lives.

In the church tradition, teaching can remain faithful to the risen Christ when it is set in the context of congregational worship (Col. 3:16-17; cf. Eph. 5:17-20). When the community is at worship, it is open to the Spirit and can recognize and teach faithfully under the claim of Jesus Christ without the stigma of arrogance or superiority. It is Jesus who must increase. The teacher is the servant of that Teacher.

Teaching Codes

Let us now look at identifiable codes and bodies of teaching material in the New Testament to explore the role of teachers in the church. The purpose of the teaching materials, judging by their nature, was to equip the church for the new life that it was called to embody within its present order. The teachers gave the gospel shape and form in the daily life of the faith community; they were the community's guides. In brief terms, if the apostles were preachers who sought the response of faith and prophets were community builders who made vivid the reality of hope, teachers were those who sought the embodiment of the gospel in daily life. That embodiment, if encapsulated in one word, was love. Such definition, while risky, provides the primary focus. "Now faith, hope, and love abide, these three; and the greatest of these is love" (1 Cor. 13:13). If we are to take Paul's words seriously, we might see the work of Christian teachers as most highly esteemed, not only in the gospel tradition, but in the apostolic tradition as well.

The problem that the teachers face, then, is the structuring of the gospel in such a way that it might have an impact on daily life. The teaching tradition is an attempt to say what the gospel claims—the gospel applied to the issues of life and the practice of faith. Fundamentally, the teaching tradition is the structuring of the gospel so that it impacts life.[13]

Paraenesis, to advise or counsel, is the common designation of the ethical material shaped by the teachers. While the word is not a significant biblical word, it does describe a style of teaching common in the Hellenistic world, a down-to-earth, intimate style of moral counsel. The purpose of the teaching tradition is to develop a new lifestyle for the community. Luke 6:27-36, which provides an example of such structuring, exemplifies the catechetical teaching tradition. Rom. 12:9-21 and 1 Pet. 3:8-12 also illustrate the method.[14]

The Lucan passage begins with the command to "love your enemies" and closes with "Be merciful, just as your Father is merciful" (6:27, 36). In between it pivots on "Do to others as you would have them do to you." Clearly, we have the love command repeated in a threefold way, undergirding the passage and creating the whole continuity and foundation. The three structural statements are "Love your enemies" (v. 27), "Do to others as you would have them do to you" (v. 31), and "Be merciful, just as your Father is merciful" (v. 36). The communication of the meaning of this command is the goal of the passage. The teachers are interpreters and communicators of this imperative.

In looking at Luke 6:27-28, we see that we have a double parallelism:

> Love your enemies,
> > do good to those who hate you,
> bless those who curse you,
> > pray for those who abuse you.

If "love your enemies" is not clear, it can be articulated as "Pray for those who abuse you." Comparison with the Matthean parallel suggests that the addition of the middle elements, "Do good to those who hate you" and "Bless those who curse you," are an elaboration within the teaching tradition of the church of the original saying, resulting in four ways of stating a relationship to be carried out by the community of faith (plural you) toward antagonists. It is the community, not individuals, that is addressed and its love is claimed.

After this fourfold presentation of the basic command, the catechetical tradition has brought into this structure a second set of statements. It is clear that these statements had a different locale in the teaching tradition because they shift from the plural to the singular you, have a different form and syntax, and are ordered differently in the Matthean parallel.

They provide specific applications of the basic stance, furnishing examples of the basic affirmation:

Positive   If anyone strikes you on the cheek,
                     offer the other also;

Prohibition	and from anyone who takes away your coat do not withhold even your shirt.
Positive	Give to every one who begs from you;
Prohibition	and if anyone takes away your goods, do not ask for them again. (Luke 6:29-30)

This set of antithetic parallels keeps the Christian ethic from generalization, gives specific shape to what it looks like to "love your enemy," and is a historically concrete instance.

The danger in Hellenistic ethics, as well as our Protestant ethic, is abstract generalization. The teacher of the biblical code gives the ethic concrete applicability. In reverse, the specific is kept from legalism. It is not a law in itself but an embodiment of the command, a descriptive example—"This is how it might look." The ethic is not confined or limited to what is described here but forces the hearer to take seriously the concrete implications of "Love your enemies."

Amazingly, the specific catches the radical nature of the command "Bless those who curse you." The response does not balance the action—it is not a reaction—nor does it follow the natural tendency to reciprocate. The shock is that the concrete neither says "take it stoically" nor "respond in kind." It opens up the possibility of a third alternative. To respond in kind makes the initiator of the action the ultimate determiner of the disciple's behavior. The alternative does not give authority to the initiator of the action, making that person the prime mover, nor does it counsel "Take it because you cannot do anything against the mover's superior power" or "Fight back and enter the relationship on the same level at which it has been initiated."

Nor does the response suggest stoic detachment from the initiator's petty concerns. The ethic does not appeal to one's self-image as being a great soul, above such petty behavior. It does not disdain.

The specific response is shocking because it hints at a new reality not embraced in the previous two alternatives. It is the existence of this new reality, the present power of God, that makes an alternative action possible. The pivotal section of the passage, "Do to others as you would have them do to you," reminds and reinforces the teaching motif that is being developed, lest the focus be lost. By itself, the Golden Rule suggests only the pragmatic mutuality characteristic of Hellenistic ethics, that is, the way you treat others will determine how they treat you. As we would say, "Treat people like adults, and they will act as adults. Parent them, and they will respond like children." Treat people positively and they will be positive. The golden rule for reciprocity of behavior characterizes Hellenistic ethics. However, the context here, in what precedes and follows, requires that it be interpreted in the style of ethic being developed. How you wish to be dealt with by others is on some basis other than reciprocity, as what follows makes clear.

We now return to a neat patterned structure:

a)   If you love those who love you,
b)   *what credit [grace] is that to you?*
c)   *For even sinners* love those who love them.
a')   If you do good to those who do good to you,
b')   *what credit [grace] is that to you?*
c')   *For even sinners* do the same.
a")   If you lend to those from whom you hope to receive,
b")   *what credit [grace] is that to you?*
c")   *Even sinners* lend to sinners, to receive as much again. (Luke 6:32-34; emphasis added)

The triplet developed deals with motivation. It suggests that the natural motivation is "to love those who love us, do good to those who treat us kindly, and to lend where there is hope of return." While such action is not to be despised, it is not enough to express the fullness of the gospel. Clearly, there is no grace in the practice of mutuality or reciprocity. That is the primary basis of Hellenistic and humanistic ethics. Mutuality is not enough—society deals in that. Mutuality is not bad or to be despised—but the gospel ethic is more radical. It is a call to go beyond. Acting for mutual benefit is basic in much that we do; it suggests how we naturally relate to friends or potential friends—not to enemies. Natural responses are adequate for friendships, but they are not for those other cases where persons are not good or friendly.

The catechetical structure, continuing the issue of what motivates love for enemies, positively affirms so radical a call. To this point we have only had inadequate or negative examples. "But love your enemies, do good [to those who hate you—implied], and lend, expecting nothing in return" (Luke 6:35). Again, mutuality or reciprocity are not adequate. Radical action is called for. What now follows is the motivation that enables you to "love your enemies": "Your reward will be great, and you will be children of the Most High; for he is kind to the ungrateful and the wicked" (6:35). The motivation to love enemies is the relationship with a God who has loved enemies—the ungrateful and the wicked. The motivation is the desire to be God's children, but that desire means nothing if one does not know the Most High to be kind (*chrestos*) to those who are evil and without mercy. The authority that gives new motivation and claim lies in relationship with God and is based upon the divine action. As such, the "reward" is not a motivation or payment but is the very relationship, as children, that the desired behavior already expresses.

The contrast is simple: either one seeks human rewards through mutuality or one's life is centered in God so that one also reaches out to enemies and the alienated, resulting in a rewarding relationship with God.[15]

The end of the passage repeats the thematic statement—"Be merciful, just as your Father is merciful" (Luke 6:36)—lest we forget what the discussion authorizes. Yet there has been movement. From the basic command, "love your enemies," we have moved to a final statement that includes a motivation for action based on knowing and calling God, "Father." This conclusion even transforms the middle structural element of the Golden Rule into a radical affirmation of "love your enemies," since you will want them to love you while you are their enemy.[16]

In summary, we have the shorthand of the Christian ethic "Love your enemy" stated several ways so we might grasp it. Specific cases are given so the command does not remain abstract, and above all, motivation is thoroughly developed, so that we might be *empowered to live and embody it out of a sense of authority and strength rather than a feeling of helplessness and weakness.*

This suggests that the essentials involved in teaching are: clarity of the ethical command; the ability to give it shape and form in concrete and historical situations; careful dealing with the motivation for the command to ensure that it carries the full power and the authority of the gospel; awareness of the parent-child relationship with God that undergirds all and forbearance from moralistic imperialism on the part of the command giver; and gospel teaching that is not informational but lays a divine demand on the hearer and the believer.

In Romans 12 we have a similar pattern of catechetical development. The passage begins: "Bless those who persecute you; bless and do not curse them" (14).[17] This exhortation is restated twice more in the passage, achieving a similar threefold thematic statement: "Do not repay anyone evil for evil, but take thought for what is noble in the sight of all" (17) and "Do not be overcome by evil, but overcome evil with good" (21). Here again it is the third statement that seems to extend the original to its full limit. Verses 15 and 16, which lie between the first two statements of the theme, suggest that the exhortation can be fulfilled only when one is embraced in a support community that rejoices with those who rejoice and weeps with those who weep (15).

Such support seems as necessary here to undergird one who will act as relationship with God was necessary in Luke to motivate the prescribed action.

This fullness of relationship is described further and given meaning in verse 16: "Live in harmony with one another [*think the same toward one another*]; do not be haughty [*think* not on uplifted things], but associate with the lowly; do not claim to be wiser than you are [do not be conceited]." Such is the concrete description of one who would and could not repay evil for evil. Further description of this posture is given in verses 18-19: "Live peaceably with all. Beloved, never avenge yourselves." Again, the love command is repeated three times.

In this function the teaching tradition only carries on the classical role of teaching in the tradition of Israel. Teaching gives shape to life by organizing and structuring the wisdom either inherited from the ages or derived from the prophetic leaders. In a basic sense, teachers are dependent upon the work of prophets and apostles in much the same way as love is rooted in one's faith and in hope (conviction) in the ultimate end and destiny of all. On the other hand, the teacher has the responsibility of relating these issues to the concrete ones of living in today's world. The teacher codifies the meaning of faith and hope for present life. The teacher gives the gospel shape and form so that it relates to the structure of present society as well as calling it to transformation.[18]

Conclusions about Teaching in the New Testament

The basic issue then is how Christian teachers structure the gospel in relation to everyday life. While *love* may be the word used to sum up the lifestyle, it is shorthand that can have meaning only if one knows the whole structure implied by it. The teaching tradition is the church's interpretation of the love command as well as its embrace of it. Teachers define love, and the way they shape the definition becomes normative in the tradition and allows for no misinterpretation. The purpose of teaching is to let the gospel speak to life by defining and developing the relationships that are shaped by the new age.[19]

In developing the specifics of the ethical catechisms, there is always the danger that the model descriptions of behavior will be understood as legal demands and norms. Such a consequence can only happen, however, when the exhortations have lost their roots in the understood and experienced reality of a relationship to God as the grace-giver, the blesser of the one who curses, and the lover of the enemy. When that reality is lost, what was theonomous, a law arising out of a living and known shaping reality, becomes heteronomous, an externally imposed law separated from the understanding and meaning of the life of the hearer and therefore seen as arbitrary.

Most often, the fear of legalism has kept us from relating ethics to historical life. As a result, we tend to talk about ethical universals and principles. Such talk floats above the unique and divergent moments of historical occurrence and gives the appearance of ethics without shaping the moment. While biblical ethics must be expressed in broad and embracing statements, they also need to be shaped and structured for the occasions of everyday life. That is the work of New Testament teachers.

Theology, especially Christology and worship, does and must undergird the work of Christian teachers. The teachers are not divorced from the achievement of the apostles or the faith of the community. The ethic that shapes the life of the community is motivated by the story of God as narrated by the apostles. It is the narrative of God's mercy to the sinner, as shown in Jesus Christ. It is the story of the Christ forgiving his persecutors, of overcoming evil with good. This keeps teaching from legalism, while enabling the teacher to clarify what it means to be a follower of Jesus Christ.

The work of teachers is not primarily eschatological. It is related to the present and seeks to shape the present form of the church's life, yet it must be guarded from conformity to the present. It is an attempt to embody now the new age that the prophet has already announced. The Holy Spirit, who brings in the new age, already calls the teachers of the church to give form and body to that promise and vision. The teachers are those who shape relationships in the present to conform to the Spirit and to the promise of that new age. Every catechetical piece rests in an eschatological framework. So the structure of the longer teaching codes always ends with an eschatological announcement.[20]

The teacher in the New Testament church was deeply concerned with motivation, ensuring that action stemmed from the gospel and not from another source. The authoritative power of the ethical claim was rooted in the relationship with God that prophets so carefully guarded. New Testament ethics are rooted in theology and in the practice of worship. It is only when Jesus is known as Lord in worship that one can live "in the Lord" as Christian ethics demand. Jesus' reign establishes absolute ethical claim. Baptism is the incorporation of the believer into the Christian life, where growth to maturity as a new person in Christ becomes possible.

Meaning for the Church Today

Teaching has suffered in the church in that it has been understood as a technical function or skill. This follows a dominant social understanding and pattern that influenced the church as well. Teaching required objectivity and consequently focused on information and facts. Being a disciple means being a perpetual learner—one who needs to be continually taught to live under the daily claim of God. To be a Christian teacher requires evangelical passion—a commitment to the faith and the hope of the gospel and a passionate desire to relate that to all the issues of present-day life. It cannot deal with back there facts nor with noncommittal spiritual values and ethics.

Teaching has meaning in the church only when it is lived in the context of that kind of worship where the authority of the

Lord is affirmed and known. The Christian life gains its power and authority as a life "in the Lord." It is impossible to choose the life of the new age now when the present-day rulers (such as economic success or peer pressure) are enthroned as lords of one's being. Only when the new Lord is enthroned in one's devotion can life of the new age be freely chosen. Only then is the power of contemporary political and social pressure broken so that one can be released from overriding fear, and the life of the new age can be embodied now.

Teachers are every bit as important in the church as apostle-preachers and prophet-community builders. The teacher's unique function is to interpret the gospel in terms of daily life, so that the reality of the gospel can be embodied now.

The sole teachers in the church are Jesus Christ and the Holy Spirit whom he has sent. Christians have the permanent status of disciples. Hence, there is reluctance to call persons teachers even after the death and resurrection of Jesus. Disciple is the preferable name. Where the title teacher is used, it must be done with care and the full understanding that it is the revelation of God in Jesus Christ that is to be communicated in the act of teaching. The disciple-teacher is always dependent upon the authority of Jesus Christ for the teaching and is open to the Holy Spirit, allowing the claim of God to be heard in the present day world, especially as a life-claiming and shaping ethic.

4

Pastors as Shepherds

In the list of identifiable leadership roles in the New Testament, the word *pastor* (the same as *shepherd*) appears comparatively late in Ephesians: "The gifts he gave were that some would be apostles, some prophets, some evangelists, some pastors and teachers" (4:11). The term shepherd is entirely absent in reference to church roles in the Letters of Paul. The verb *to shepherd* (tends a flock) occurs only once in Paul (1 Cor. 9:7), and there it is a literal reference. As those who herd the flock get some of the milk, so the apostle is worthy of support. The rest of the New Testament references to shepherds, shepherding, and flocks are limited in number and widely scattered, although some are in very crucial places, such as Paul's farewell speech to the elders of Ephesus and the shepherds at the birth of Jesus in Luke-Acts and in Jesus' discourse in John 10.

Old Testament Roots for the Image

The root for this leadership image goes back to ancient culture, especially in the Old Testament. The shepherd boy,

David, was chosen by God to be ruler (1 Sam. 16:11-13). That boy, as a shepherd and not a warrior, delivered Israel from the taunting and militantly powerful Goliath. Out of this model the Old Testament develops the powerful analogy of the ruler and the shepherd. In many ways this analogy is deeply rooted in the image of God as the one who shepherds: who feeds, leads, protects, and cares for God's people (Psalm 23). The image of the ruler as shepherd is nourished and developed by the prophets (Jer. 23:1-4) who discover that the rulers never fulfill their role as shepherd. Ezekiel 34 gives the fullest picture of this: The shepherds of Israel have been feeding themselves, living off the flock instead of feeding it (2-3, 8, 10). The shepherds have not strengthened the weak, nor healed the sick, nor bound the crippled, nor sought the lost (4, 16). And they have acted with force and harshness in ruling the sheep (4). As a result, the sheep have been scattered, the flock dissipated and lost, becoming the prey for all the wild beasts (5-6, 8).

Zechariah continues this judgment against the shepherds; the rulers after the exile are worthless shepherds: "My anger is hot against the shepherds" (10:3); "Awake, O sword, against my shepherd" (13:7). Ultimately, to lack a shepherd is to die (11:4-17). Because Israel has rejected God, the leaders abuse the people. God will require his sheep at their hands.

Since human shepherds fail, God will seek the lost sheep; God will gather and feed them (Ezek. 34:7-16). God will be the true Davidic shepherd (Isa. 40:11; Jer. 50:19; Mic. 7:14) and will appoint better shepherds (Jer. 3:15). The divine shepherd role is to gather the scattered sheep into a community and to feed them. The shepherds are feeders, waterers, and care givers—persons who build community.

The failure of Hebrew monarchs to care for the people and their temptation to lord status over them kept any specific historical ruler from ever being labeled as shepherd.[1] Shepherd becomes the specific title for the Davidic Messiah only.

Jesus as the Shepherd in the Gospels

We will discuss the scattered New Testament references to shepherds in the order of their completeness, realizing that they belong to the later non-Pauline writings. The most vivid narratives depicting Jesus Christ as the true shepherd occur in the various stories of the feeding of the multitude. Shepherds are, of course, primarily feeders, so that Jesus is fulfilling the pastoral role in this act.[2]

The Gospel of Mark

In Mark 6, before the feeding, Jesus is described as: "He saw a great crowd; and he had compassion for them, because they were like sheep without a shepherd; and he began to teach them many things" (34).[3] The crowd is like shepherdless sheep, fainting with hunger. Jesus responds with compassion, first exercising pastoral leadership by teaching.[4] They are in the wilderness, the place of hunger, of temptation by Satan, and always, therefore, the place of potential death. It is here that Jesus *gathers* and *feeds* the shapeless, scattered people who are without identity. The crowd (*ochlos*) is a picture of society, not the church.

The disciples, overwhelmed by the operational task, want to dismiss the shepherdless crowd, so that it can do its own foraging. But Jesus commands the disciples, "You give them something to eat" (6:37). The disciples still do not comprehend their "pastoral" role in society or the deeper level of the discussion, and so they can only reflect on their limitations: "Are we to go and buy two hundred denarii worth of bread, and give it to them to eat?" (37). They are more aware of sociology than gospel. They make decisions on the basis of statistics, not the wondrous power of the gospel.

Nevertheless, the role of the disciples is emphasized, and when the broken loaves are set before the people, they are agents of the divine action. They are to be feeders.

Jesus, drawing heavily on imagery from the Exodus, commands the company to sit down by hundreds and fifties. He gathers and orders the scattered flock on the grass. In this act he is bringing order in the midst of the chaotic crowd (cf. Exod. 18:13-27), and using the human resources at hand, he took, "blessed and broke the loaves, and gave them" (Mark 6:41). The language of this feeding reflects the language of the Lord's Supper (Mark 14:22-25), where Jesus interpreted the cross as the great act of feeding. The positive meaning of the cross is rooted in an act of shepherding.

This meal is an experience and foretaste of the Messianic Age. Messianic imagery predominates. Yet God's compassionate feeding has already begun through Jesus' pastoral act and the disciples' participation in it.

The result of this feeding is that all were filled and there was adequate food left over to distribute to the widows and the orphans.[5] The feeding grace of God does not run out or diminish.

Mark 6:52 makes clear that the disciples do not understand what this story is about. Understanding will come only after the Lord's Supper and the cross and Resurrection. The disciples are not yet broken open to the power of God and true feeding (cf. 4:33-34). The story is followed by a discussion with the disciples in the boat, which makes clear that they still do not understand the nature of the feeding (Mark 8:14-21). Their hearts are hardened. They do not understand. In their literalism they think the leaven of the Pharisees is something they eat.

Matt. 9:36 also describes Jesus as compassionate when he saw the crowds "because they were harassed and helpless, like sheep without a shepherd." To this confused multitude he sends the disciples to teach (Matthew 10). Again teaching is the basic nature of the pastoral office. Elsewhere, pastoral compassion has to do with healing the sick (Matt. 14:14; 20:34; Mark 1:41), or raising the dead (Luke 7:13). In the teaching of Jesus, compassion characterizes the attitude of the Good Samaritan (Luke 10:33), the father of the Prodigal Son (Luke 15:20), and the lord who forgave his servant a large debt (Matt. 18:27).

The only other use of shepherd in Mark occurs in the decisive remark of Jesus following the Lord's Supper: "You will all become deserters; for it is written, 'I will strike the shepherd, and the sheep will be scattered'" (14:27; from Zech. 13:7).[6] His death means the destruction of the companionship of the disciples and their flight. The promise that follows is intriguing: "But after I am raised up, I will go before you [*proaxo*] to Galilee" (Mark 14:28). This image describes the promised risen Christ's appearance in Galilee as the act of gathering the scattered flock and establishing a new relationship that can no longer be broken by death.[7] This is supported by Mark 16:7 where the youth at the tomb repeats the same words with the promise that the disciples will see him in Galilee. Such a gathering of the disciples around a new presence parallels Zechariah where God gathers a new people after the scattering of the old (13:9). Thus, the Resurrection gathers the disciples around a new center of loyalty, the risen Christ, and therefore death can never again break the new relationship, which is characterized by worship.

So in a limited but decisive way Jesus is interpreted as a true shepherd who nurtures the people with his teaching; who orders the disordered crowd and has compassion on all sorts of persons in deathlike situations (hunger in the wilderness, the sick, and the dead); whose death as shepherd results in the scattering of the disciples but with the promise that they will be gathered again; and whose ultimate destiny implies that they shall be participants in his pastoral ministry.

The Gospel of John

The image of Christ as shepherd-pastor is developed in John 10:1-18. In these verses the noun *shepherd* is used five times and *flock* once. These words occur nowhere else in this gospel so that this chapter, while crucial in figure, is unique in John and may well reflect a general church tradition.[8]

The passage has three dominant contrasting images; the good shepherd contrasts with strangers, thieves, and hired hands. The shepherd calls the sheep by name; they know his voice and respond. He leads them out and goes before them; they will follow. They but do not know the voice of the stranger and so they will not follow, but flee from the stranger. Strangers do not know the sheep by name, that is, they are neither personally related to the sheep nor do they care about them. In a certain sense they are the "cold professionals." Big oil does not know me by name; the electronic church does not know me by name.

The risen Jesus knows Mary and calls her by name. In that act the relationship broken by death is restored (John 20:16; cf. RSV 1:48 where Nathaniel, confronted by Jesus, responds, "How do you know me?"). Throughout John Jesus fulfills the role of the shepherd. He knows his own by name.

The good shepherd provides pasture and feed for the sheep. He not only enters by the door, but in a mixed image, he becomes the door through which the sheep are brought to pasture. By contrast, the thieves and robbers are not interested in nourishing and nurturing the sheep. They are there to feed themselves, to devour. They are "consumers" who use the shepherdless mass for their own gratification. They profit by the lack of gathering or community among the flock. They characterize a society geared to consumption.

A good shepherd lays down his life for the sheep. The death of Jesus achieves the gathering action of a true shepherd (cf. John 11:51-52). By contrast, the hireling flees because the hired hand is motivated by the pay, and the job is not profitable when a price has to be paid to care for the sheep. The hireling's motive is profit, and the amount of pay alone gives identity. However, the Good Shepherd is willing to pay the price of his own death for the sake of the sheep.

In John 10 Jesus is the gatekeeper who gives passage, the leader who knows them and who goes before them to make the way, the life-giver who lays down his life, and, finally and climactically, the gatherer.

Jesus as Shepherd in the Rest of the New Testament

In a much more limited way the prophet John, in the Book of Revelation, wondrously describes the Lamb as a shepherd who nourishes persons to life: "For the lamb at the center of the throne will be their shepherd, and he will guide them to springs of the water of life" (7:17). What a reversal from the rulers whom Ezekiel saw devouring the flock, not seeking the lost or strengthening the weak, or from the thieves and robbers in the Gospel of John. He, the Lamb who bears all, is the true shepherd ruler. He is the good, the model shepherd. However, the stress on a shepherd's caring must never blunt the sense of the Good Shepherd's rule and authority. For those who reject his shepherding for their own devices, he will shepherd with a rod of iron (Rev. 12:5; 19:15; cf. 2:27). The shepherd, in church usage, is a figure of authority with definite functions. The issue is not whether the shepherd has authority—that is clear—but to rightly use that authority. It is the caring function of the pastor that limits and clarifies the nature of authority. Human shepherds always used their power for their own point of view and advantage.

In 1 Peter the function of Christ is shepherd in two places. He is "the shepherd and guardian [*episkopos*] of your souls" (2:25) and "the chief shepherd" (5:4). The hymn in 1 Peter presents a vivid picture of the role fulfilled by Christ. The climactic affirmation that Jesus is "the shepherd and guardian of your souls" patterns the ministry of Jesus after that of the suffering servant of Isaiah 53:

> "He committed no sin, and no deceit was
> found in his mouth."

> When he was abused, he did not return abuse; when he
> suffered, he did not threaten; but he entrusted himself
> to the one who judges justly. He himself bore our sins
> in his body on the cross, so that, free from sins, we
> might live for righteousness; by his wounds you have
> been healed. (1 Pet. 2:22-24)

Shepherding is suffering servanthood, or, in John's words, the
readiness to lay down one's life for the sheep.

Church Leaders as Pastors and Shepherds

In 1 Peter 5 the elder calls colleagues to model the Good
Shepherd who is acclaimed in the hymn in chapter 2. However,
the whole congregation is expected to model its life after the
Shepherd Messiah: "For to this you have been called, because
Christ also suffered for you, leaving you an example, so that you
should follow in his steps" (2:21). The shepherd role for church
leaders and for the congregation is rooted in the pastoral action
of the Lord. Disciples now share in the shepherding task exercised by Jesus Christ. Jesus' shepherding action in the hymn is
their model for ministry (2:22-25).

Similarly in the Gospel of John, the risen Christ uses the
symbol of shepherd to commission Peter for pastoral leadership
(21:15-19). Peter and the disciples are to be shepherds. Peter is
to be a feeder of the flock, but the necessary priority for pastoral
authority and ministry is love for the Lord. Three times the
question "Do you love me?" is repeated (21:15-17). An affirma-
tive answer is prerequisite before one can become God's shepherd. Ultimately, Peter will glorify Jesus in death, recalling the
Good Shepherd who lays down his life for the sheep. The call of
Peter reflects two of the Good Shepherd's qualities: caring (not
devouring) and self-giving (not a hireling).

This image of pastoral leadership is reflected throughout
the later New Testament and is apparently the reason why pastor

appears in the list of church leaders in Ephesians. In Acts 20 Paul makes his farewell speech as a free person on his way to Jerusalem. In his charge to the Ephesian elders he admonishes, "Keep watch over yourselves and over all the flock, of which the Holy Spirit has made you overseers [*episkopoi*, supervisors], to shepherd the church of God" (28). Shepherding is the image for church leaders. By contrast, they are warned that wolves will come, not sparing the flock (29). Again we see that wolves plunder even as the rulers of Israel had done in Ezekiel's day (chap. 34).[9] By contrast, shepherds supervise and feed.

The leaders of the congregation, as shepherds, are to protect the congregation from those who speak perverse things—heresy—in order to get a personal following (Acts 20:30). Consequently, false leaders divide and plunder and do not gather the community. By contrast, Paul did not use the church or covet the members' possessions, but he supported himself and by toil helped the weak (20:33-35). The one who "pastors," feeds, the flock may be an elder, as in this passage, or a bishop, or deacons. The deacons are literally those who wait on tables, feeders concerned with food distribution (Luke 22:26-27 and Acts 6).

The word *to look over* or *to supervise* (*episcopos*), later translated as *bishop*, is continually used in describing the function of Christian elders. The shepherd-pastor exercises the function of looking over the congregation. That means passionate interest in the congregation, discerning what is happening. Thus, they are commanded to be alert to discern both the congregation and the action of God (Acts 20:31). The life of the congregation depends on having a faithful one looking over it, that is, teaching it, admonishing it, and nurturing it, and by such means ruling it.

Similarly, the elder writing 1 Peter charges the other elders "to tend [shepherd] the flock of God that is in your charge, exercising the oversight [*episkopeo*], not under compulsion but willingly, as God would have you do it—not for sordid gain [greed]), but eagerly. Do not lord it over those in your charge, but be examples to the flock" (5:2-3). Again, the shepherd's role stresses acting neither out of self-gain nor in domination. They are instead to exercise care among equals. Domination, of course, is using and plundering the flock. It scatters and devours as do false shepherds. Rather the shepherd becomes the exemplary leader among the flock.

True pastoral rule involves nurturing and feeding those who have lost their way. It is giving meaning to the disoriented crowd. Its goal is to gather persons together into community. As the Johannine prayer expresses it: "That they may be one" (John 17:11). The pastor is the gatherer.

Pastoral service is characterized by compassion for the helpless, who can be plundered easily; pastoral service is relating closely or "knowing them by name"; it is paying the price when there is no prospect for a return. This is the antithesis of the hired hand. The bottom line is that the sufferer, the one who cared when it cost to do so, is the only one who can be the true and trusted leader and who can guard and model in some small way the ministry of Christ. What is distinctive is never power over sheep but intimate knowledge of and love for them.

On the contrary, where care is absent, dominance (1 Peter), force and harshness (Ezekiel), plunder (Acts), avoidance or lack of relations (John), or false teaching (Acts) occur. When all the dimensions of this picture are viewed, we get a good listing of the sins of wolves, strangers, and hirelings, who masquerade in shepherds' clothing.

The title *elder*, more commonly *pastor*, is used to describe the shepherding role of ministry. As such, a current Jewish title has been filled with new meaning (cf. 1 Clem. 54:2).[10] Elders shepherd and supervise. Elder is one of the terms that the church uses to describe the role of pastor. That usage also helps account for the minimal use of the title pastor. Pastor is mainly an image that is identified with other titles—elder, overseer, and even deacon. Supervision (*episkope*) is a function for overseers and elders.

The Relation of Pastors and Teachers

The teaching character of the pastoral function seems to support the listing in Eph. 4:11 (see the discussion of Matt. 10:1 and Mark 6:30ff. earlier).[11] The absence of a repeated article suggests that the phrase "some pastors and teachers" refers to a single group of persons. Such a suggestion further augments the discussion of teachers in the previous chapter, where teachers are those concerned with love, nurture, and care. The development of the image of pastor, then, would seem to be a special development encompassing the teaching function of early church leaders and combining with it the function of rule or administrative care.

This identification of pastor as teacher seems to reflect what we see in the activity of Jesus himself. When he saw the crowds harassed and helpless like sheep without a shepherd (Mark 6:30-34), his act was to feed; but as we have seen, the first "food" was taught. This priority helps clarify the gospel's emphasis on teaching, which is a nurturing process.

Above all it makes clear the development reflected in the pastoral Epistles. They are concerned with the "feeding" offices in the church—bishops, deacons—and they put great emphasis on teaching and what is taught. Sound teaching is the recurrent theme in the Pastorals (1 Tim. 1:3; 6:2-3; 2 Tim. 1:13-14; Titus 2:7-8). The function of the "Timothys" that are to carry on Paul's work is "rightly explaining the word of truth" (2 Tim. 2:15; cf. 4:2-3). False teaching is called such things as "godless chatter," "senseless controversies," "speculations," "quarrels over the law," and "myths" and "endless genealogies," while the persons who employ such are "empty talkers" and "deceivers."[12]

When the relation between shepherd and teaching is evident, then the modern title *pastoral Epistles* seems to be a responsible description of the nature of these second generation writings concerned with the pastoral roles of bishops-elders-deacons-widows as those responsible for sound teaching and nurture in the church.

The Relation to Other Titles for Church Leaders

While the pastoring role in ministry is clear and secure in itself, it is described by several other titles in the New Testament. The terms *bishop*, *elder*, and *deacon* do not express clearly distinct functions in the New Testament but are various ways in which the function of pastor-teacher is described. Eventually, the term *minister* comes to be used for this pastor-teacher function, just as the specific offices of the bishop, elder, and deacon develop because the image of shepherd was not common to Hellenistic urban life.

Acts and 1 Peter talk about the function of elders as overseers and shepherds. The word translated as *shepherd* or *guardian* in Acts 20:28 and 1 Pet. 2:25 and 5:2 refers to the work of the bishop. Guardian (*episkopos*) is in parallel construction with shepherd (1 Pet. 2:25), indicating that these two terms are parallel and refer to interrelated activity. They describe a function of pastoral ministry. Overseers in the Hellenistic world or Qumran[13] and elders in the Jewish community each held definite social leadership roles. These leadership titles were being filled with new and Christian meaning—the role of the shepherd. Overseeing or supervising is not dominating, as Gentiles do, but shepherding.

Dominating or *lording it over* is used just four times, but there are also several related uses of the less intense word *to lord*, which also means *to dominate*. In addition to the usage in 1 Pet. 5:3, which we have already discussed, "dominating" is used in Mark and Matthew as a stern rebuke to James and John's request for chief seats. Jesus' rebuke reads,

You know that among the Gentiles those whom they recognize as their rulers lord it over them, and their great ones are tyrants over them. But it is not so among you; but whoever wishes to become great among you must be your servant, and whoever wishes to be first among you must be slave of all. (Mark 10:42-44; Matt. 20:25-27)

By contrast, when the seven sons of Sceva acted presumptuously, the evil spirit "leaped on them, mastered them all, and overpowered them that they fled out of the house naked and wounded" (Acts 19:16). Lording over others is a fitting act for an evil spirit but deserves rebuke when it is a tactic employed by disciples. The less intensive form is used in Luke's dispute over greatness. "The kings of the Gentiles lord it over them; and those in authority over them are called benefactors. But not so with you; rather the greatest among you must become like the youngest, and the leader like one who serves" (Luke 22:25-26). Both here and in Mark 10 it is serving (*diakoneo*) that characterizes the true role of leadership. Disciples, like Old Testament rulers, are tempted to corrupt pastoral rule into domination, copying the pattern of authority in much of society and culture.

The word minister (*diakonos*) gathers within itself some of the dimensions of shepherding. It is a new image shaped in the early church but with a meaning similar to shepherding. It moves from the literal image of serving tables, rather than sitting at them (Luke 22:27), to speak of giving one's life as a ransom in a pivotal passage in Mark 10:45, or feeding the neglected widows in Acts 6:2. Already in Paul's ministry this word for serving tables is used to describe the offering that Paul takes for the poor in Jerusalem (Rom. 15:25). Paul also calls the offering the great act of "sharing in this ministry to the saints" (2 Cor. 8:4). It is a grace being ministered for the glory of God (2 Cor. 8:19), a generous gift being administered (8:20), a service for the saints (9:1), a ministry overflowing in thanksgivings to God (9:12), a test of ministry glorifying God (9:13).[14] Climactically, that ministry is one of reconciliation, but the specific act of reconciliation is feeding, caring, and nurturing the poor of Jerusalem (Rom. 15:26).[15]

The Greek word *to watch over* (*episkeptomai*), which relates to our word *bishop*, helps to clarify the interrelation of these terms.[16] It means *to watch over*, and therefore *to care for*. As such, it can suggest *to examine* or *to investigate*, but it also came to mean *to visit the sick or those who need care*. Discipline and care are combined in this word.[17]

In the Septuagint, the meanings develop along these same lines. From looking on or investigating the word comes to express concern or care as well as supervision. It could be used of the shepherd and sheep, as in "shepherds who shepherd my people" (Jer. 23:2), or a "shepherd who does not care for the perishing, or seek the wandering, or heal the maimed, or nourish the healthy, but devours the flesh of the fat ones" (Zech. 11:16, see also Ezek. 34:11, 12). In Num. 27:17 the Lord God is to look out for (*episkeptomai*) a person who will lead the flock in and out, lest they be a sheep without a shepherd (cf. Mark 6:34). So we see that the shepherding images identified in the Old Testament are immediately connected with the functions of watching over, visiting, or supervising (*episkopeo*). God's visit to followers can mean supportive love, but God's watching presence also means examination and even judgment on those who are alienated from God (Zech. 10:3).[18]

In the New Testament *overseeing* with the sense of positive care and appropriate discipline is reflected in Moses' decision to visit his relatives in Egypt (Acts 7:23) as well as when Paul and Barnabas determine to visit the churches to see how they are (Acts 15:36).[19]

This redefining of roles is patterned on the character of God who watches over, guards, and visits the people of God for their salvation (Luke 7:16; Acts 15:14). The same God also laments that Jerusalem does not know the day of "visitation" (*episkope*, Luke 19:44). God's caring, nurturing presence is not perceived.

Finally, the whole sense of God's guardianship, supervision, and scrutiny can be embodied in a specific person, function, and perhaps even an office. In the Septuagint *episkopos* denotes a wide variety of persons in authority, such as army officers, building supervisors, business managers, and city officials.[20] So Eleazar is appointed over the tabernacle and its vessels (Num. 4:16). The seven servers (deacons) in Acts are appointed, set to watch over, the tables as an official function. Here the act of appointing (*episkeptomai*) is to fulfill the ministry (*diakonia*) of tables (feeding) (Acts 6:3).

In an unusual passage, Paul mentions bishops or overseers and deacons who are singled out as special persons in the congregation (Phil. 1:1). While the modern position of bishop was not in mind, Paul does know persons in the church at Philippi who function in leadership roles that we might translate as supervisors and assistants (cf. 1 Thess. 5:12).

The second formal mention of supervisors-overseers in the New Testament occurs in 1 Timothy, which describes the qualifications of bishops and deacons (3:2; Titus 1:5-7). The lack of the reference to both bishops and elders in the Pastorals suggests that at this time overseer and elder were not different offices but rather were two ways of describing the pastoral function for the early church. Elders may well be the official title, with *episcopos* defining what the function is (Titus 1:5-7). The final mention is in Acts where Paul addresses the elders at Ephesus as overseers (Acts 20:28).[21] Such persons exercise authority for the benefit of the community. They are to fulfill the office that the rulers of Israel always perverted in their power so that they could never truly be called shepherds.

In the qualifications given for an overseer in 1 Timothy, "He must manage his own household well" characterizes the temptation to church leaders as well as Hebrew rulers (*proistemi*; 1 Tim. 3:4, 5, 12; 5:17; Titus 3:8, 14). This is not a practical requirement of household management that one must pass to be a leader in the congregation, as if church leaders were to be skilled in business management, rather it is another form of the expression of true rule and parallels the image of watching over. It was easy for fathers in Hellenistic society to lord it over their families because of the male cultural role, and if they cannot manage (*proistemi*) their own families, they will not be able to care for (*epimelomai*) the church (1 Tim. 3:4-5).[22] In other words, males who dominate their families cannot be leaders in the church.

J. H. Elliott clarifies the relationship of elder to overseeing. Bishops must not be recent converts (*neophutos*). They are to be mature in faith, not necessarily in age (1 Tim. 3:6; 4:12), lest they be puffed up and domineering, which is the temptation that accompanies too quick a rise in prestige and power. The younger in faith are to be subject to the elders in faith (1 Pet. 5:5), for the whole concern is that young converts grow into maturity (1 Pet. 2:2-3). Even Peter could shepherd when he was younger (John 21:18). Conversely, however, true leaders regard themselves as no more important than recent converts: "The greatest among you must become like the youngest" (Luke 22:26; cf. John 13:1-20).[23] The younger, it seems, do the menial tasks (Acts 5:6, 10). Other qualities of bishops, elders, and deacons in the Pastorals reflect the concerns we saw in John 10: they must not be "puffed up with conceit" (1 Tim. 3:6), "greedy for money" (3:8), or "arrogant or quick-tempered or addicted to wine or violent or greedy for gain" (Titus 1:7). Such actions do not build community. On the positive side, a leader is "hospitable, a lover of goodness, prudent, upright, devout, and self-controlled" (Titus 1:8; cf. 3:8, 14).

Those who teach "for sordid gain" upset families and are insubordinate to the Word of God (Titus 1:11). Sound teaching is always the mark of pastoral leadership.

While Paul does not use to oversee or visit, and refers to supervisors and deacons only in Phil. 1:1,[24] twice in the teaching sections of his letters Paul has used the verb *proistemi*, to stand before or to manage, to suggest leadership functions in the

Christian community. Paul lists the function without identifying the office. Interestingly, this word, like *to watch over*, means *to rule*, but combines within it the meaning of *to care for*.[25] Because of immediate context, the RSV translates Rom. 12:8 as "he who gives aid, with zeal," but the word means much more, suggesting rule as "managing the family." Leading and caring for are united by Paul in this special word. Käsemann comments, "As in 1 Thess. 5:12 it may be to various organizational tasks including the founding of house churches and the settlement of disputes" that it refers. "Since this is a thankless task, they are called to *spoude* or total dedication."[26] The same word in 1 Thess. 5:12, the earliest Pauline letter, is translated by the NRSV as "respect those who labor among you and are over you [manage or rule] in the Lord." It could as well be translated "respect those who labor among you and care for you in the Lord and admonish you." The phrase "in the Lord" defines the context for this pastoral exercise of authority and responsibility.

In reverse, Rom. 12:8c (RSV) should be heard not only as the one "who gives aid [cares], with zeal," but also with the overtones, the one "who rules, with zeal," or better, the one "who exercises caring rule, with zeal." This brings teaching, prophecy, and caring rule (pastoring) in close proximity in Rom. 12:6-8. These are the local church leadership functions. Here Paul provides the basis for leadership in a word used elsewhere only in the Pastorals, and there of bishop-shepherds. The pastoral description is much closer to Paul at this point than is usually supposed.

Finally, in Corinthians one of the gifts of the Spirit is identified as *kubernesis* (governing). The word literally refers to the helmsman who directs the ship and secular usage applied it by analogy to the statesman and the ship of state. In 1 Corinthians it refers to the gift of the Holy Spirit that qualifies a Christian to steer the congregation. Side by side in the Corinthian list are the gifts of support (of defense and aid given by a higher authority) and gifts of guidance for steering the church. Help and guidance are characteristics of congregational rule.

Further, the local church leaders, elders-supervisors, who develop as the administrators in the local congregation must then be agents of the pastoral function or pastors in actuality. They are the shepherds of the congregation, and whatever their specific tasks, they are to serve as the feeders and the gatherers of the community.

The Congregation as the Shepherded Flock

Finally, a brief word about the image of the congregation as a flock is in order. The flock does suggest weakness, potential lostness, and overdependence on the shepherd Lord (Matt. 10:6; 15:24). The Good Shepherd does exercise a saving action toward the lost (Matt. 18:12-14; Luke 15:3-7; John 10:10). At the same time, however, members of the flock are the recipients of divine grace (Luke 12:32), and they are a people gathered together in community. Being gathered together out of their scatteredness is a gift that caring leadership bestows. To be a flock is to have a new identity and to belong to a community. So the affirmations of the Psalmist hold: "We are the people of his pasture, and the sheep of his hand" (Ps. 95:7; cf. 100:3; 79:13). To be the flock is to be a people in God's possession and care. However, as in covenant, to abuse or reject that relationship is to experience also the shepherding rule of God in judgment.

The flock always requires care and nurture. Only an atoning death nurtures a flock as a people of God's care. While the word *church* is not used by John, Mark, and Luke, they do refer to the people of God as the flock, intimately bound in identity to its shepherd, so that this way of speaking of the church makes clear its identity in relation to the Lord. They know him and are known; they trust him and hear him. The connotation of flock conveys much more than the word church. It is not a word that demeans; it identifies the church as people gathered and formed by God's graceful, nurturing act, rooting the community in the rule of the Good Shepherd.

Conclusions Concerning
Pastors in the New Testament

There is an amazing thread best described as pastoral supervision—exercised by people with a variety of titles or with no title—that runs through all levels of the early church. Titles, when used, are from both the Hellenistic and Jewish environments. Dimensions of pastoral care and supervision have been added to the titles or they are derived from images of leadership, but they have been modified by emphasizing supervision for the sake of caring and support.

The title of elder now includes careful supervision to discern issues and needs within the congregation. It reflects somewhat the role of the overseer or bishop, the watching and supervising leader.[27] Being an elder also encompasses the shepherding and feeding function, including serving, teaching, and seeking the lost, which the title of pastor fully expresses. So titles are filled with meanings that derive from the strong emphasis on the pastoring mission of the early community.

There are temptations, such as vanity and arrogance, that come to those who exercise caring rule. The shepherding dimension of the leadership role is always a reminder that one is there to feed others, to act as servant, even while one is called to maturity in faith and discernment of the needs of the community. The goal of pastoral ministry is to lead persons to maturity. Such growth includes the ability to exercise care in each other's behalf, discerning the needs of all.

Preaching within this context aims at deepening individual commitments and rekindling the will to serve God, lest believers become indifferent to God's way. It addresses equals in God and calls upon them in familiar terms to develop day by day the resources and awareness of the meaning of Christian life. This preaching, of course, serves the goal of growth and maturity in the congregation.

The distinction between so-called charismatic and universal ministries and local and institutional offices does not reflect the New Testament understanding of leadership. The terms elder, bishop, and deacon all reflect one basic understanding of leadership that is carried best in the image of shepherding or pastoring. It is the careful understanding of the pastoral role that keeps other roles from becoming corrupted by power.

The roles of pastor and teacher seem to interchange and intertwine. Part of the feeding role is teaching in the church. Teaching becomes the most important expression of pastoral care, nurturing the congregation that it might grow into full obedience and faith in the Lord. Pastors, by their teaching, exercise their caring function for the community, and so fulfill a ministry that reflects Christ's. Ministry expresses the shepherding role of the New Testament church leader both as one who teaches and one who exercises care.

The church as a community also shares responsibility for the teaching and nurture of the whole of society. Because this pastoral care characterizes the church established by Jesus Christ, it can also be seen as a special gift for the leaders within the congregation. This ministry exists so the congregation may exercise its necessary responsibility in society.

The Meaning for the Church Today

The New Testament community has a clear and specific understanding of pastoral rule and authority. Often the understanding of contemporary ministry, as in the figure of the enabler, does not make that authority and rule clear. All local pastors are overseers, guardians, and caring rulers in the best sense.

Christian rule can easily be perverted by secular concepts; the temptation in pastoral leadership is to dominate rather than minister. The function of rule is caring for by teaching and nurturing, even while the corollary is a teaching discipline. In the church today we have difficulty bringing together caring for and calling the church to accountability. True shepherds not only gather the chaotic fragments of society into a community, but they can supervise the congregation, discern its character, and discipline the elements that are disruptive and threatening to the community. Disruptive leaders include cold professionals (John's strangers), consumers who live off society without contributing to it, and hirelings who work only when it is profitable. Above all, true shepherds can discern and oppose false teachers.

The consolidation of pastor and teacher into the same person as intimated in the Ephesians list is something that has happened in the church. In these forms the local congregational leadership was being shaped. *To shepherd* was expressed as much by nourishing with teaching as by caring for the sick or feeding with food. Ministry gets its meaning from overseeing care, shepherding, guarding, watching over, and visiting. To shepherd (*poimano*), to oversee (*episkopeo*), and to stand before (*proistemi*) are interrelated and define the caring ministry of the pastor-teacher.

Pastors will never recover their identity in the church until they see themselves as teachers of the faith. True pastoral care is not primarily in the psychology of counseling or the sociology of food distribution but in nurturing faith by careful teaching. The loss of identity in the modern church is characterized by the loss of a teaching pastor.

The goal of the teaching pastor is to cause an existing congregation and people to mature—to grow up in the Lord. As the apostles and prophets deal with faith and hope, the pastor-teacher nurtures through teaching care and discipline. For the pastor to fail to rule correctly harms the whole church. Pastors are not necessarily prophets or apostles. There are diverse gifts of the Spirit. But they are responsible in the church for a particular form of rule. While apostles tell the story of God's mighty act in the past and prophets look for the new age, pastor-teachers live in the present, seeking to have the gospel embodied in the life of the congregation. Pastor-teachers are local leaders who exercise the greater gift and task of love, as espoused by Paul, in the congregation's mutual ministry.

5

Ministry

We conclude with a brief look at the use of the words *minister*, *to minister*, and *ministry* (*diakonia* and related words). Their use in the New Testament community is as varied and as ambiguous as in the contemporary church.

The verb *diakoneo* literally means "to wait on tables" or "serving food." A number of New Testament references reflect this basic activity, generally by a slave (cf. Luke 12:37; Acts 6:2). As such, the noun form is an appropriate term for those persons who have responsibility for feeding the community, however that act may be understood. When ministry is used to describe caring for the community, it describes the role of pastor-teachers, including the work of bishops and deacons.

However, it is also clear that the word *diakonia* (and its related verb) means something much broader than distributing food; it may even be used to describe the general work of leadership in the New Testament community. This is most clearly evident in Acts 6:4 where, after seeking to be relieved of the large task of ministering tables, the disciples indicate that they would devote themselves "to prayer and to serving the word." This begins to provide a broader framework in which the church understands ministry beyond the limited function of deacons. It reminds us of the shepherding of the multitude by Jesus where he begins his feeding by teaching. So Paul includes an apostle in the larger task of ministry (Rom. 11:13; cf. Acts 1:25 where ministry and apostleship are interrelated) as well as describing the ministry of the collection he is taking for Jerusalem (2 Corinthians 8). Acts, too, describes Paul's work as ministry (20:24; 21:19). The fundamental meaning of the word *to serve tables* carries with it the understanding that the lesser person serves the greater. It is this meaning that vividly grasps what the life of Jesus is about: "The Son of Man came not to be served but to serve, and to give his life a ransom for many" (Mark 10:45).

The same understanding is also reflected in Luke's account of the Last Supper when Jesus talks about the meaning of his death. The disciples have been at their favorite subject again, debating who is the greatest. Jesus responds:

> The kings of the Gentiles lord it over them; and those in authority over them are called benefactors. But not so with you; rather the greatest among you must become like the youngest, and the leader like one who serves. For who is greater, the one who is at the table or the one who serves? Is it not the one at the table? But I am among you as one who serves. (22:25-27)

The word that sums up the action of Jesus' life equally describes the general posture of Christian leadership. The task of leadership is to serve. Ministry, then, refers to the work of Christian leaders in general, who are not to lord it over others, but who are to serve so that others might become greater. Paul and Apollos are servants who plant and water; God gives the growth (1 Cor. 3:5; cf. 2 Cor. 11:23 where the idea of serving Christ carries this same sense of little ones serving another). So Paul has the general task of ministry by the gift of God (2 Cor. 4:1; Rom. 1:1). It is also called a ministry of the Spirit, a ministry of righteousness (2 Cor. 3:8, 9), and a ministry of reconciliation (2 Cor. 5:18). All of these describe ministry in its full breadth of building up the community of faith and enabling persons to grow into the family of God.

Surprisingly, though Paul talks about prophets and lists teachers in the basic listing of gifts of ministry, he never calls any of his many companions by title except those also designated as apostles. Rather, he uses the larger term ministry and by so doing embraces all the things that they as leaders have in common, namely, their commitment to enhance others, not themselves. The identifiable gifts and functions of ministry are never used by Paul in a competitive way.

He also uses relational words to describe the commonality between all those who labor independently but often in contact with him for awhile. So they are associate workers (Mark, Aristarchus, Demas, and Luke in Philemon 24; cf. Col. 4:10-11) and brothers (Apollos in 1 Cor. 16:12). Paul also associates *diakonos* with the general term of "co-worker" (1 Cor. 3:5, 9; 2 Cor. 6:1, 4).[1]

Paul does not distinguish grades in the functional ministries but clearly sees them as sharing in importance. His use of titles, or lack thereof, indicates that he accepts diverse ministries as the workings of the same Spirit, all being necessary for the life of the community. He personally deals with persons in the broader terms of co-worker, brother, and minister. The total perspective is that all these leadership roles serve the larger purpose of increasing others through work and service. The minister, assuming the role of servant, seeks the greatness of the other.

To engage in this ministry means that the table servers need to believe seriously in the way Jesus has already forged as servant (cf. Luke 22:27) and which is interpreted through the Lord's Supper to be the meaning of Jesus' death. The serious believer, who makes no self-claims at the table, is in no way forgotten nor rejected in the ultimate relationship with God (John 13:1-16). On the contrary, to wash the disciples' feet is the very foundation of Jesus' lordship and teaching authority. To serve the other means to share in the rewards of the resurrection age—which certainly cannot be understood as earthly rewards (Luke 14:12-14). One is to take the place of a servant, knowing that God values and lifts up those who do not vaunt themselves (14:7-11). In Luke, especially, the way one relates to the table and the companions who gather there determines how one relates to God and God's rule. One either lays claim to place and demands one's just dessert, as is the habit of society, or one serves others, even as Paul ministers to the church at Jerusalem, and in the act of service becomes an integral member of the Christian community. In so doing one also binds one's communities to Jerusalem and the Jerusalem community to the Pauline community (2 Cor. 8:13-15).

Finally, there is a third dimension of meaning of ministry that is still larger in scope. The term not only describes a specific form of ministry, deacons, and it not only describes all church leaders who seek to bring the increase of life to others, but it also describes all Christians, who, by virtue of belonging to the community of God's people already living toward the new age, live for the good of the neighbor. In this sense Paul uses service, ministry, not only to describe apostles, prophets, and teachers but also to include all kinds of more general, less ecclesiastically directed, forms of service (1 Cor. 12:5), including the utterance of wisdom, gifts of healing, and the working of mighty deeds.

The ultimate gift that undergirds and transforms all gifts of service is love (1 Corinthians 13). Without love all gifts degenerate into self-centered arrogance with no value (13:1-3). Active love[2] is the reality of the coming rule of God, which is already at work in the present. Love is the new age invading and transforming this society. Love never falls flat (13:8). Ultimately, all church members, by virtue of their calling in baptism, must embody the ministry of human concern that lives for the well-being of others. The whole community must finally learn and embody that which is the specific concern of pastors-teachers, namely, caring love. In so doing they not only fulfill their identity as disciples-learners, but they also bring to fruition the work of the teachers who labor so that the prophetic gospel of hope might be lived and realized in the present and the faith called forth by the preaching of the gospel of Jesus Christ might ultimately work through love in the life of the world.

NOTES

Introduction

1. Eduard Schweizer, *Church Order in the New Testament*, trans. Frank Clark (Naperville, Ill.: A. R. Allenson, 1961), 171.
2. *Archon* can denote demonic powers in the New Testament, and *leitourgos* is used once by Paul, in Rom. 15:16, about himself. Otherwise, it refers to Roman government officials, to priestly service in the Old Testament, and to Jesus Christ's own service (Heb. 8:2-6). The single Pauline use stands alone and functions symbolically of his bringing the offering of the Gentiles' praise to God.

Chapter 1

1. Karl Heinrich Rengstorf identifies this as unique to the verb *apostello* where emphasis is on the commission attached to the sending. With the noun *apostolos* (the primary use in the New Testament), again the stress is on the person who is

109

sent in full authority (Gerhard Kittel, ed., *Theological Dictionary of the New Testament* [*TDNT*], trans. and ed. Geoffrey W. Bromiley [Grand Rapids, Mich.: Eerdmans, 1964], 1:404, 421).

2. In 2 Cor. 8:23 Paul identifies "apostles of the churches," which suggests a general usage of the one sent by the community. So also, Epaphroditus is described as the Philippians' apostle to Paul's need (Phil. 2:25). Philippi is the sender, and Paul is the recipient.

3. It has been suggested that the phrase is ambiguous and need not infer that Andronicus and Junias were apostles. In either case the apostles are a clearly marked body. The plain sense suggests that Andronicus and Junias were apostles. Ernst Käsemann observes that it means "prominent among them" (*Commentary on Romans*, trans. and ed. Geoffrey W. Bromiley [Grand Rapids, Mich.: Eerdmans, 1980], 414). Cf. Rudolf Schnackenburg in "Apostles Before and During Paul's Time," in *Apostolic History and the Gospel*, ed. W. Ward Gasque and R. P. Martin (Exeter: Paternoster Press, 1970), 293.

4. Käsemann identifies them as Jewish Christian missionaries, perhaps from Antioch (*Romans*, 414).

5. *Appointed* describes God's act of creating something new as embodied in giving Israel a new role (Rom. 4:17; Gen. 17:5) or in God's reducing the ruler's enemies to a footstool (Mark 12:36; Acts 2:35; Ps. 110:1). The Holy Spirit appoints guardians in the Ephesian church who are to shepherd the church of God. The most direct use of the word to describe God's appointive act is in John 15:16 during Jesus' final speech to the disciples. Jesus makes clear that he is appointing them and choosing that they bear fruit.

6. Schnackenburg, "Apostles," 287-303.

7. Reginald H. Fuller, *The Formation of the Resurrection Narratives* (Philadelphia: Fortress Press, 1980), 36-42.

8. Cf. 1 Cor. 12:6 and 12:11 where it is God who energizes the special ministries that are apportioned (*diareo*) in the church.
9. The verb is used in Rom. 10:15, "How are they to proclaim him unless they are sent"; 1 Cor. 1:17, "Christ did not send me to baptize but to proclaim the gospel"; and 2 Cor. 12:18, where Paul talks of sending Titus to Corinth.
10. Paul seems to include Timothy as an apostle, i.e., preacher of the gospel, though he did not see the resurrected Christ (1 Thess. 2:7). Another possible qualification of the resurrection appearance for apostleship lies in the identification of Andronicus and Junia as apostles (Rom. 16:7). They were apostles before him and it may be that in the Hellenistic church there was already a route to apostleship, beyond that of an appearance, as a basis for being a witness to the Resurrection. It is possible that these persons' experience goes back to the early days in Jerusalem. Hans Von Campenhausen and James D. G. Dunn see that apostleship is ended with the appearance to Paul. He is the last of the apostles. His monstrous or untimely birth is a prematurity. He was called to apostleship in an unusual appearance, without knowing the historical Jesus, lest apostleship be closed before he was there. Such a view suggests a limited concept of apostleship from the beginning, later limited to the founders as is suggested by the Lucan or Ephesian development. The later tendency is implied by references also in Revelation (2:2), the Didache (11:3-6), and Hermas' *Similitudes* (9.15.4), where apostles are still conceivable in communities where limiting the term to the "founders" has not yet occurred. The movement toward restricting the term to the founders is understandable because the apostles' witness is foundational (*Ecclesiastical Authority and Spiritual Power in the Church*, trans. J. A. Baker [Stanford, Calif.: Stanford University Press, 1969]; *Jesus and the Spirit: A Study of the Religious and Charismatic Experi-*

ence of Jesus and the First Christians as Reflected in the New Testament [Philadelphia: Westminster, 1975]).

11. Walther Schmithals, *The Office of Apostle in the Early Church*, trans. John E. Steely (Nashville: Abingdon Press, 1969), 32-37.

12. Charles Kingsley Barrett, *The First Epistle to the Corinthians* (New York: Harper & Row, 1968), 110.

13. John Howard Schutz, *Paul and the Anatomy of Apostolic Authority* (London: Cambridge University Press, 1975), 242ff.

14. Barrett suggests that the conflict in Galatians 2 "with those who were of repute" centers on this issue. He suggests that "pillars" is the name given apostles in Jerusalem, suggesting the importance of the new age (Luke 22:29-30). For Paul the only foundation is Jesus Christ. Yet for Paul they are always important as links to the new age and companionship and consultation are to be maintained ("Paul and the Pillar Apostles," in *Studia Paulina,* ed. J. N. Sevenster and W. C. Van Unnik [Haarlem: E. F. Bohn, 1953], 1ff.).

15. Von Campenhausen, *Ecclesiastical Authority*, 47, and Dunn, *Jesus and the Spirit*, 278-80.

16. Where there is no word of the Lord, Paul gives his understanding but does not claim it as the voice of God. His apostolic authority is grace given, but that does not mean his words are inspired by the Spirit (charismatic). What he does say of his utterance is: "And I think that I too have the Spirit of God" (1 Cor. 7:40).

17. Rengstorf, *TDNT*, 1:418-19.

18. Schutz, *Paul and the Anatomy*, 206ff.

19. Ibid., cf. 40-42 for an extended discussion of the gospel and its relation to the apostle.

20. Ibid., 103.

21. Rengstorf, *TDNT*, 1:446. Paul's understanding of *apostle* is much more permanent than that of the Jewish *shaliach*.

22. Cf. Rom. 14:9 where the formula is related to lordship. Lord is the title appropriate to expressing relationship to the community of faith in worship (Werner R. Kramer, *Christ, Lord, Son of God*, trans. Brian Hardy, Studies in Biblical Theology [Naperville, Ill.: A. R. Allenson, 1966], 72f).
23. Ibid., 39ff.
24. John Andrew Kirk understands that the usage in Mark 6:17 has no apologetic motive; therefore, the term goes back to Palestine and to the original setting of Jesus in the Gospels ("Apostleship Since Rengstorf: Towards a Synthesis," *New Testament Studies* 21 [January 1975]: 259).
25. There is a variant reading that names the Twelve also as apostles when they are appointed in Mark 3:14. The purpose of the appointing there is "to be with him, and to be sent out to proclaim the message, and to have authority to cast out demons." Such a function indicates why either Mark or the scribe adds the additional phrase, "whom he also named apostles." Martin Hengel points out that the prototype for the call of the apostles to this function is in the call of the prophets where the prophetic call is indicated by *being sent* (*apostello*) in the Septuagint (Isa. 6:8; Ezek. 2:4; 13:6; Exod. 3:10-15; 1 Sam. 15:1; Jer. 19:14; 25:17; 26:12) (*The Charismatic Leader and His Followers*, trans. James Greig [New York: Crossroad, 1981], 83).
26. The appointment of the Seventy parallel to the Twelve would seem to suggest no limitation on apostleship, although Luke does not give them the name of apostle.
27. That identification is only in Heb. 3:1.
28. Rengstorf, *TDNT*, 1:405.
29. Ibid., 404.
30. This usage stops in Acts 20, but in the structure of Acts 21 through 28 is the defense of Paul against the authorities, which provides a different model: he is the pattern for Christians who are called to give a faithful apology against

the church's detractors and persecutors. Here Acts develops Paul the apologist, not Paul the apostle.

31. Karl Heinrich Rengstorf, "The Election of Matthias," in *Current Issues of New Testament Interpretation*, ed. William Klassen and Graydon F. Snyder (New York: Harper & Row, 1962), 178-92.

32. Ibid., 192.

33. Schuyler Brown, "Apostleship in the New Testament," *New Testament Studies* 30 (July 1984): 479.

34. However, the Didache still refers to itinerants called apostles, so the development is not uniform (11:1-3; 15:1; cf. Rev. 2:2).

Chapter 2

1. Paul only uses the verb *to prophesy* in 1 Cor. 11-14. This suggests that the roles of prophet, apostle, and teacher are clearly identifiable.

2. This ties back to 1 Cor. 13:5, where love "does not insist on its own way." Similarly, "If I come to you speaking in tongues, how will I benefit [*opheleso*] you" (14:6) verbally recalls 13:3, "but do not have love, I gain [*opheloumai*] nothing." Chapter 13 undergirds the judgments of chapter 14.

3. Ralph P. Martin sets forth the possibility of reading the indicative, "You desire the spiritual gifts," to which Paul responds, "I will show you a still more excellent way" (1 Cor. 12:31) (*The Spirit in the Congregation* [Grand Rapids, Mich.: Eerdmans, 1984], 34ff.). David Aune suggests that the higher gifts are presumably the first three on the list: apostles, prophets, and teachers (*Prophecy in Early Christianity and the Ancient Mediterranean World* [Grand Rapids, Mich.: Eerdmans, 1983], 199).

4. Wayne Grudem, *The Gift of Prophecy in 1 Corinthians* (Lanham, Md.: University Press of America, 1982), 118ff.

5. But it must be remembered that prophecy, while disclosing the eschatological purpose of God, still is a this-worldly function. So the prophet sees "in a mirror, dimly" (1 Cor. 13:12). The reference to "if I have prophetic powers, and understand all mysteries and all knowledge" does suggest that prophecy, ideally, is the disclosure of the divine mystery and, hence, the revelation of God's new age (1 Cor. 13:2).

6. 1 Cor. 13:2 seems to associate prophecy and mystery: "And if I have prophetic powers, and understand all mysteries and all knowledge . . ."

7. Aune, *Prophecy*, 211.

8. Grudem, *Gift*, 129.

9. Cf. 1 Cor. 11:29-31 where the community fails to discern the Lord's presence (4:7); 1 Cor. 6:5 continues with the expectation of critical discernment within the congregation.

10. Cf. 1 John 4:1ff. where the community "tests" the spirits; cf. 1 Cor. 2:13-14. Gerhard Dantzenberg suggests that prophets can "discern" the Spirit; it is a charisma. The community can test it (*Urchristliche Prophetie: ihre Erforschung ihre Voraussetzungen im Judentum und ihre Struktur im ersten Korintherbrief* [Stuttgart: W. Kohlhammer, 1975], 132).

11. Cf. Grudem, *Gift*, 63-67, for a discussion of the possibilities of how this evaluation could take place in the Corinthian community. Aune suggests that Num. 11:29 is so interpreted by the rabbis that prophecy is seen as the sign of the new age (*Prophecy*, 193).

12. Cf. Rev. 22:6, "The God of the spirits of the prophets."

13. Cf. Jacob Jervil, *The Unknown Paul* (Minneapolis: Augsburg Publishing House, 1984), esp. chap. 7, "The Center of Scripture."

14. David Hill presents an extensive discussion of John as a prophetic book in *New Testament Prophecy* (Louisville: Westminster/John Knox Press, 1979), 70-87. This includes an extensive analysis of prophetic forms in Revelation.

15. "I know your works [I know you] . . . But I have this against you . . . Remember . . . Repent and do."
16. Cf. Matt. 11:15; 13:9, 43; Mark 4:9, 23; Luke 8:8; and 14:35 where Jesus summons, "Let anyone with ears listen!"
17. Cf. Hill, *New Testament Prophecy*, 87-93.
18. Eugene Boring, "The Influence of Christian Prophecy on the Johannine Portrayal of the Paraclete and Jesus," *New Testament Studies* 25 (October 1978): 113-23. Boring would see the description of the functioning of the Paraclete as being in an identifiable group who are endowed with the Spirit. Further, the gospel reveals the same chain of command, "The Paraclete / whom I will send / to you / from the Father" (cf. John 14:26), as was reflected in the opening verses of Revelation.
19. Cf. Mark 6:15 and 8:28 regarding the identification of Jesus as a prophet by others.
20. All the Old Testament prophets quoted in the New Testament are speakers of the word of the Lord. They reveal his will and purpose to the human community. Often this is literally expressed by the phrase, "through the prophet" (Matt. 1:22; 2:15).
21. Compare the interchange of terms in Acts 10:14-15, 19; also 2 Cor. 3:17-18.
22. Just such a lack of distinction in the Hellenistic world created the specific problem that Paul faced in Corinth (1 Cor. 12-14). Paul is forced to make distinctions because while he accepts both as possible gifts of the Spirit, prophecy alone expresses concern for the building of the community. However, Hill would understand Luke here in the same light as Acts 2:4ff. They spoke in "other languages," "that is in various [foreign] languages which would be understood by the hearers with a view to the proclamation of the wonderful works of God" (*New Testament Prophecy*, 97-98). Hence, Acts 10:46 and 19:6 may mean, as in Acts 2,

the intelligible communication of the gospel that characterizes prophecy.

23. This is paralleled in Matthew's Sermon on Mission,
where the Spirit is fundamental to courageous witness
(10:16-20). This whole understanding seems to derive
from the eschatological setting where one learns to
live by the new age as the old order is given away. The
persecutions are but the "birth-pangs" of the new (Mark
13:8-13).

24. It is a word unique in Acts, occurring four times. It describes
Paul's activity in revisiting the congregations to *strengthen*
them (18:23; 15:41; 14:22). Hence, it describes the prophet's
task of building up the church. In fifteen uses of *oikodomeo-* in
Luke-Acts, only once is it used in the figurative sense of
building up the church.

25. James L. Martyn notes the understanding that the Christology of John develops from a "prophet like Moses" to that
of "the coming of the Son of Man" (*History and Theology
in the Fourth Gospel*, 2nd ed. [Nashville: Abingdon Press,
1979], 91-142). It is this pilgrimage in understanding that
the gospel seeks to foster.

26. A large part of the accusation and condemnation of Jesus
seems to treat him as a prophet, charging him with being
a false one. When he does not reveal who struck him while
he was blindfolded (Luke 22:64; Matt. 26:68; Mark
14:65; cf. Luke 7:39), he is accused of being a false
prophet because of his inability to disclose that which is
hidden.

27. Compare Matt. 23:34 with 23:29. Compare also Matt.
13:17 and 10:41.

28. David Hill, "*Dikaioi* as a Quasi-Technical Term," *New
Testament Studies* 11 (April 1965): 296-302.

29. That "fight the good fight" means fearless confession
before persecutors seems indicated when the phrase is used

along with the remembrance of Jesus' good confession (1 Tim. 6:13) before Pontius Pilate (cf. Matt. 10:17-20).

30. Cf. Paul Minear, *The Commands of Christ* (Nashville: Abingdon Press, 1972), chap. 9. Much of what is here presented was stimulated first by Minear.

31. Ibid., 157-64.

32. "Pray without ceasing, give thanks in all circumstances. . . . Do not quench the Spirit. Do not despise the words of prophet" (1 Thess. 5:17-20).

33. Cf. Didache 10:7; 15:1.

34. In terms of 1 Thess. 5:10, he is secure, "so that whether we are awake or sleep we may live with him."

35. Compare Matt. 25:1-13 and 24:37-43 for other uses of some of the same imagery. Signs of something new are vividly given; but they too demand their own form of insight (Matt. 24:32-33).

36. E. Earle Ellis develops the interrelation extensively in "The Role of the Christian Prophet in Acts," in *Apostolic History and the Gospel*, ed. Ward Gasque and Ralph P. Martin (Exeter: Paternoster Press, 1970), 58ff.

Chapter 3

1. Karl Heinrich Rengstorf's definition of *didasko* in *Theological Dictionary of the New Testament* (*TDNT*) (ed. Gerhard Kittel, trans. and ed. Geoffrey W. Bromiley [Grand Rapids, Mich.: Eerdmans, 1954], 2:137).

2. Rengstorf's definition of *mantheno* (*TDNT*, 4:402, 404).

3. Raymond Brown, *The Churches the Apostles Left Behind* (New York: Paulist Press, 1984), 91-93.

4. John describes Jesus as teaching in five other places. The Jews also sarcastically ask, "Would you teach us?" (9:34 RSV). John does not use the term to describe the disciples' activity.

5. Rengstorf, *TDNT*, 2:143. In 1 John 2:27 it is the baptism of God or the Holy Spirit that "teaches you about all things, and is true and is not a lie, and just as it has taught you, abide in him."

6. In Matt. 26:18 Jesus calls himself teacher in a command to the disciples to prepare the Passover. The text follows the parallel in Mark at this point. The closest any of the disciples come is when Judas twice addresses him as "rabbi" in the betrayal (26:25, 49). Six times the vocative *teacher* is used by others in Matthew. By contrast, Jesus was addressed as teacher in Mark four times (4:38; 9:38; 10:35; 13:1).

7. Jack Kingsbury, *Matthew*, Proclamation Commentaries: The New Testament Witness for Preaching (Philadelphia: Fortress Press, 1977), 8.

8. The verb occurs fourteen times in Matthew and seventeen times in Mark; the noun occurs three times in Matthew and five times in Mark.

9. Matt. 28:15 refers to the way the guards at the tomb did as they were told in spreading the rumor that Jesus' body had been stolen.

10. The only other use is in Rom. 2:20, where it is in an indictment against Jewish teachers for not living up to their teachings.

11. From 1 Corinthians 14 we sense that teachers and prophets are local church leaders. Revelation parallels prophecy; knowledge parallels teaching (14:6, 26). Observe Acts 13:1 for further depiction of local church functioning.

12. Cf. 1 Cor. 12:4-13:13, where community building is rooted in the extensive teaching section about love.

13. Cf. Dale R. Allison, "The Pauline Epistles and the Synoptic Gospels: The Pattern of Parallels," *New Testament Studies* 28 (January 1982): 1-32. This article develops the common elements in teaching collections in the Epistles and in the

Gospels, especially Romans 12-14; 1 Thessalonians 4-5; Colossians 3-4; 1 Corinthians 7, 9, 11, 14; Luke 6:27-38; and Mark 9:33-50 and 6:6b-13. He concludes that Paul knows the teaching traditions passed on in the Christian community that are rooted in Jesus.

14. 1 Thessalonians 4-5; 1 Corinthians 12-13; 1 Pet. 2:11-4:11; Romans 12-13; and Ephesians 4-6 indicate larger units of structured ethical tradition in the Epistles.

15. Cf. Matt. 6:1-13, where the relationship with God, not being seen by persons, is the motivation for action. "In secret" is the way of affirming the priority of God. See Paul Minear, *The Commands of Christ* (Nashville: Abingdon Press, 1972), chap. 3.

16. The Didache, as the teaching tradition continues, loses the radical gospel motivation and returns to pragmatic, humanly intelligible motives for the love command. "Love those who hate you and you will have no enemy" is a counsel for success (1:3); "If anyone would take your goods, do not ask them back, for you are not able" no longer comprehends the surprising and amazing action and power of God but confirms and affirms the Christian's feeling of weakness and powerlessness by a counsel of futility (1:4).

17. Previously in Rom. 12:9ff we have had a description of the Christian life rooted in love. The following verses (9-13) develop hypocritical or false love.

18. Cf. Rom. 12:1-2, which is the call that introduces the perspective of the ethical section. See also 1 Pet. 1:14-15.

19. 1 Pet. 3:8-12 is in a different biblical strata that makes a similar impact. It sums up the catechetical material begun in 2:11 and brings it to a close. Verse 9 finally gathers all the previous material into an embracing statement on life: "Do not repay evil for evil or abuse for abuse; but, on the contrary, repay with a blessing. It is for this that you were called—that you may inherit a blessing." While many

ethical facets have been previously covered, the central theme has always been in sight.

20. Rom. 13:11-14; Col. 4:2-4; Eph. 6:10-20; and 1 Pet. 4:7-11.

Chapter 4

1. Joachim Jeremiah's definition of *poimen* in *Theological Dictionary of the New Testament* (*TDNT*) (ed. Gerhard Kittel, trans. and ed. Geoffrey W. Bromiley [Grand Rapids, Mich.: Eerdmans, 1964], 6:487-88).

2. Mark 6:34; see also Mark 8:1-10; John 6; Matt. 14:13-21; 15:32-39; and Luke 9:10-17.

3. Cf. Mark 8:2-3; Ezek. 34:5; Num. 27:17; and 1 Kings 22:17, where the picture of aimless people occurs.

4. This reflects the grouping of the words *pastor* and *teacher* in the Ephesians list, where the two functions seem to describe the same persons.

5. So Mark 8:19-21 suggests after Mark tells the feeding a second time. Cf. Acts 6 where the Twelve and the Seven distribute food from the common meal, "the breaking of the bread," to the widows.

6. In Zechariah it is a call to destroy the false shepherd of Israel and let the sheep be scattered. God will then purify a third and gather them.

7. Reginald H. Fuller, *The Formation of the Resurrection Narratives* (Philadelphia: Fortress Press, 1980), 58. John 10:4-5 uses a Greek phrase here, translated "He goes before them, and the sheep will follow him for they know his voice. A stranger they will not follow."

8. John 21, most likely by a different author, uses the verb *to shepherd* once and the word *sheep* twice.

9. Matthew describes false prophets as inwardly ravenous wolves (7:15).

10. Anthony E. Harvey, "Elders," *The Journal of Theological Studies* 25 (October 1974): 318-32.

11. Raymond E. Brown, *"Episkopos* and *Episkope*: N.T. Evidence," *Theological Studies* 41 (June 1980): 322-38.

12. "Godless chatter," 1 Tim. 6:20 and 2 Tim. 2:16; "senseless controversies," Titus 3:9; "speculations," 1 Tim. 1:4; "quarrels over the law," Titus 3:9; "myths" and "endless genealogies," 1 Tim. 1:4 and 4:7; "empty talkers," Titus 1:10; and "deceivers," Titus 1:10 and 2 Tim. 3:13.

13. In 1 Clement Christ does not exalt himself over the flock, as some do, but he is humble (16:1).

14. In these six uses of the word *diakonia-diakoneo*, as it describes the collection, the RSV translates it "relief" one time, "offering" once, "rendering" once, "service" once, while the verb is translated "carrying on" and "administering." The unique theological perspective that this word gives to the offering is thus diminished by these translations.

15. *Diakonos* is the general term developed to describe all types of caring, feeding ministry, although in the Pastorals it is beginning to be associated with the position of deacon (1 Tim. 3:8-12).

16. Hermann W. Beyer, *TDNT*, 6:601ff.

17. The verb *to oversee* or *visit* occurs most often in Luke-Acts. Seven of eleven uses of *to visit* (*episkeptomai*) are in Luke-Acts, two are in the parable of the last judgment, and one each in Matthew and James. The word *visitation* occurs twice in Luke-Acts, once in 1 Timothy and once in 1 Peter. The word *bishop-overseer* occurs once each in Acts, Philippians, 1 Peter, and twice in the Pastorals. The related word *episkopeo* occurs in 1 Pet. 5:2 and in Heb. 12:15. On the other hand, this language occurs only in Phil. 1:1 in Paul.

18. Beyer, *TDNT*, 6:602 (cf. Jer. 6:15; 10:15; 11:23; and Isa. 10:3, where the prophets speak of the day of visitation as a day of judgment).

19. Cf. Matt. 25:36, 43, where it describes visiting the sick and the prisoner, and James 1:27 where it describes piety as visiting (guarding) the orphan and the widow.
20. G. B. Caird, *The Language and Imagery of the Bible* (Louisville: Westminster/John Knox Press, 1980), 81.
21. In the Old Testament elders were heads of families who were leaders in local government (1 Sam. 16:4). It is the primary term from Judaism to designate a church office of leadership.
22. In the parable of the good Samaritan, *epimelomai* twice describes the Samaritan's act toward the wounded man (Luke 10:34, 35). The less intensive form (*melo*) is found in Mark 4:38: "Teacher, do you not *care* that we are perishing?" (emphasis added). Cf. Mark 12:14; Luke 10:40; John 10:13 (where it describes the acts of shepherding); 12:6 (of care for the poor); and 1 Pet. 5:7 (describing God's care for you).
23. John Hall Elliott, "Ministry and Church Order in the New Testament: A Tradition-Historical Analysis (1 Pet. 5:1-5 and parallels)," *Catholic Biblical Quarterly* 32 (July 1970): 381-83.
24. In addition, fellow-workers, those who labor, brothers, and ministers, all seem to be titles in Paul for clearly defined groups of local leaders (Earle Ellis, "Paul and His Co-Workers," *New Testament Studies* 17 [July 1971]: 437-52).
25. Beyer, *TDNT*, 6:604.
26. Ernst Käsemann, *Commentary on Romans*, trans. and ed. Geoffrey W. Bromiley (Grand Rapids, Mich.: Eerdmans, 1980), 342.
27. Raymond E. Brown discerns two offices in the local church: the higher office of presbyter-bishop and the subordinate office of the younger-deacon (cf. the parallelism of these two in Luke 22:26-27 and 1 Tim. 5:1-2) ("*Episkope* and

Episkopos: N.T. Evidence," *Theological Studies* 41 [June 1980]: 337).

Chapter 5

1. E. Earle Ellis shows that *brothers* is another special term for co-workers that Paul uses to designate a restricted group over against the total congregation, which in related verses are called *saints* and *church* ("Paul and His Co-Workers," *New Testament Studies* 17 [1971]: 446). For this distinction that the texts evidence see 1 Cor. 16:19f; Phil. 4:21; Col. 4:15; and cf. Eph. 6:26f.
2. Love in 1 Cor. 13:4-8 is described only in verbs. The translation makes it sound like an essence: "Love is . . ." Love is a verb as God is known in verbs.

262.109
W414

LINCOLN CHRISTIAN COLLEGE AND SEMINARY

87002

262.109 Wehrli, Eugene S.
W414   Gifted by their
          spirit

                    87002

DEMCO